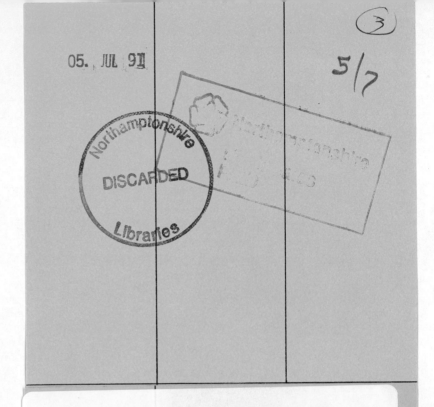

Past-into-Present Series

THE CONSERVATIVE PARTY

Peter Lane

Principal Lecturer in History,
Coloma College of Education

B T BATSFORD LTD London

First published 1974
© Peter Lane, 1974

Typeset and printed
in Great Britain by
REDWOOD BURN LIMITED
Trowbridge & Esher
for the publishers
B. T. Batsford Ltd, 4 Fitzhardinge Street, London W1H 0AH
ISBN 0 7134 1789 7

Contents

Acknowledgments

The Author and Publishers wish to thank the following for illustrations which appear in this book: Camera Press for figs 57, 60–63; Central Press Photos Ltd for fig 54; Fox Photos for figs 1, 47; GLC for fig. 46; Keystone Press for figs 50, 52, 56, 59, 64; Mansell Collection for figs 4–6, 8–10, 13, 15, 16, 20–23, 26, 28, 29, 31, 34, 35, 37; National Portrait Gallery for fig 7; *New Statesman* for figs 53, 65; Paul Popper Ltd for figs 45, 58; Radio Times Hulton Picture Library for figs 25, 27, 33, 38–44, 48, 49; Sheffield City Libraries for fig. 12; Sport and General Agency for fig. 51.

They also wish to thank the publishers who allowed quotations to be used from their books and whose names are acknowledged on the relevant pages.

The Illustrations

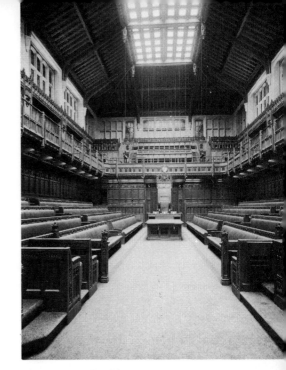

1 The interior of the House of Commons which was rebuilt after being bombed during the War (1939–45). Churchill, who was Prime Minister at the time, insisted that it should be built so that there would not be enough seats for all MPs; this gives the House an intimate atmosphere that would be missing in a larger House. Notice the two-sided design; the very shape seems to call for a two-party system

Introduction

Figure 1 is a photograph taken of the interior of the House of Commons, looking towards the Speaker's Chair. On either side of the Chair the rows of benches wait for the MPs who will take their places when Parliament reassembles. Most foreign Parliaments meet in semi-circular rooms; the British Parliament meets in an oblong-shaped room. This is important: the shape of the Commons has been one of the reasons for the British two-party system. In foreign Parliaments, with their semi-circular shape, there is no clear division between parties. In the House of Commons there is a very clear division between the two sides.

Some people think that this is a bad thing; they believe that there ought to be a large number of political parties—as there are in France and Italy. There an MP might start off as a Radical Socialist, disagree with that Party about something, and become a Radical Independent Socialist; if he then falls out with that Party he simply moves a little way around the semi-circle to become a Moderate Republican Socialist and so on round the semi-circle. In Britain, each political party is forced to become a coalition of people who, in France, might be members of different parties. Thus, in the British Labour Party there are a group of extreme left-wing MPs who find a good deal in common with Communists, a large group of moderate MPs in the centre of the Labour Party and a small group of right-wing Labour MPs who have much in common with some Conservative MPs. The Conservative Party is a coalition containing MPs who have different views on the Common Market, capital punishment, comprehensive education and so on.

You will know from reading other books that, in the past, one of the largest and most important parties was the Liberal Party. Today, as we know, the Liberal Party has only a small number of MPs: its place as the party of protest and of reform has been taken by the Labour Party which was only started at the end of the nineteenth century. But the Conservative Party remains; unlike the Whigs and the Liberals it has not disappeared.

2 In the British two-party system the Liberals had been the 'natural' alternative to the Conservatives. However, in the 1890s the Independent Labour Party, led by Hardie (the face of the Frog), made its appearance. The Ox represents the Liberal Party. But there was not room for both of them, and the Liberal party has declined as the Labour Party has grown

'The Ox and the Frog.' The Frog: 'I shall soon be bigger than you.' The Ox: 'All right, I don't mind, there's plenty of room for both of us – but mind you don't burst!'

Changing nature of Conservatism

One of the reasons for this permanence has been that there is always a need for a party which will represent those people who do not want change and reform, which will want, in other words, to *conserve* things as they are. Another reason for the long life enjoyed by the Conservatives is that they have changed their policies as the need arose. For example, in 1714 the official policy of the Conservative or Tory Party was the restoration of the Stuarts to the throne of England; as it became clear that this policy was unpopular and unlikely to succeed the Tories dropped it and became faithful supporters of the Hanoverians. In 1830 the Tories opposed the Whig policy of parliamentary reform; in 1867, under Disraeli, they proposed an extension of that reform. This willingness to learn, to change, is one which has helped the Conservative Party to remain in existence while other parties have died out.

In the course of the following pages we will trace the development of the Conservative Party from its roots in the religious struggles of the seventeenth century. In 1714 it seemed as if the Party was doomed and the Whigs would be the party of government; in 1846 the Tories split and the Liberals came to power; in 1945 some people believed that the Labour Party was set for a long period of government. We know, of course, that in 1714, 1846 and 1945 the pessimists were wrong and that the Conservative Party has not only survived but has become very much the party of government, while Whig, Liberal and Labour Parties have held office less frequently than people had expected.

3 A cartoon (1884) illustrating the split in the Conservative Party between Northcote (the traditionalist), Churchill (who wanted more social reform), and Salisbury (who pursued a policy of Empire building). In the end, the majority followed Salisbury, and Churchill was forced to retire from office

THE "PRELIMINARY CANTER."

1 Charles II to the Younger Pitt

What is a political party?

'A party is a body of men united for promoting, by their joint efforts, some particular idea on which they are all agreed. Everyone in the party will try to put men who hold their opinions into positions so that they can carry out their agreed plans with all the power and authority of the State.' This is what Edmund Burke wrote in 1770, in what has been called the first demand for a system of party government.

No parties

Burke's idea sounded almost revolutionary to the MPs and politicians of the late eighteenth century. They would have sounded nonsensical to people of previous ages. When Wolsey failed to organise a divorce for Henry VIII, the King had him arrested and replaced by Thomas Cromwell. When Cromwell displeased the King on other grounds he, too, was dismissed and later executed. In Tudor times the King really governed.

4 Edmund Burke, who presented the first argument in favour of party government. He was ahead of his time: his ideas were put into practice in the nineteenth century

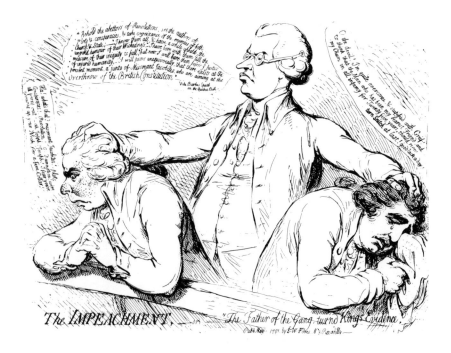

The Tudors did, of course, have Parliaments; but it was the Monarch who decided when an election should be held, which towns or villages should be allowed to elect an MP, how long a Parliament should remain in being, when it should be dismissed to await recall (a *prorogation*) and when it should be dismissed to wait for another election (a *dissolution*).

When the Monarch held such wide powers there was no chance for men to form political parties to control the government. In the 1640s the Parliamentarians waged a Civil War against the Royalists—and in one way this is the start of party activity. But this quarrel was settled by war, which is not a political solution. In any case the Monarchy was 'restored' in 1660, when Charles II was invited back to Britain with all the powers that his Tudor predecessors had had.

The beginnings of the Party in the 1670s

Charles II came to the throne in 1660, amidst a general rejoicing which led to the election of a Parliament which was very friendly to this 'Merry Monarch'. But by 1670 many MPs, and several of Charles's appointed Ministers had begun to suspect that he was trying to restore Catholicism in England. He had made an alliance with Catholic King Louis of France to fight a war against the Protestant Dutch; he had married a Catholic Princess. His brother James, Duke of York and the heir to the throne, had become a Catholic and had married a Catholic Princess, Mary of Modena.

5 Charles II (centre, seated) at the Council meeting, listening to Titus Oates presenting his evidence concerning the Popish Plot

TITUS OATES,
From a rare Print?

6 Titus Oates in the stocks. Oates had been an Anglican, became a Catholic but recanted to become an Anglican again. He had given evidence of a Popish Plot (figure 5) and the fear this had roused had been used by Shaftesbury and the Whigs to whip up popular support for their anti-Catholic policies. Oates later confessed to being a liar and this caused a reaction in favour of Charles II, against Shaftesbury and the Whigs

In 1673 Parliament passed the Test Act which insisted that 'the holder of any civil or military office should take the sacrament according to the rites of the Church of England . . . and make a declaration against the Catholic doctrine of the mass'.

This led to the Duke of York's resignation as Lord High Admiral. Meanwhile, in 1678, Titus Oates, a former Catholic, announced that he had evidence of a Popish plot to kill the King, to massacre English Protestants and to support a French invasion of England and Ireland. On 31 October 1678 the House of Commons resolved 'that there has been a damnable and hellish plot, contrived and carried on by Popish recusants for . . . murdering the King . . . and rooting out and destroying the Protestant religion'. Charles II did not believe that there was any such plot; he dismissed Parliament in January 1679 and called for an election in March. When this Parliament tried to pass the Exclusion Bill to keep James off the throne, Charles dismissed it. After an election in October 1679, Parliament was prorogued until January 1681, when it met to declare that the King could not be given the increased taxes for which he was asking until he had agreed to the passage of the Exclusion Bill. Charles dismissed this Parliament— and a third election was called for. As Macaulay wrote:

The one question of the Exclusion occupied the public mind. . . . On one side it was maintained that the constitution and religion of the state could never be secure under a Popish King; on the other, that the right of James to wear the crown in his turn was derived from God. . . . The name of Whig was given to those English politicians who showed a disposition to oppose the court and to treat Protestant Nonconformists with indulgence. The bogs of Ireland, at the same time, afforded a refuge to Popish outlaws . . . then called Tories. The name of Tory was therefore given to Englishmen who refused to concur in excluding a Roman Catholic prince from the throne.

The politicians

In the 1680s when party activity got under way there were only 160,000 voters, most of whom were under the influence of some great landowner or other. There were very few independent MPs—only about 200 or so in England and Wales according to a survey. So anyone who wanted to form a political party had to try to influence the landowners who were so important, and the 200 or so independent MPs who were not elected by the influence of the Treasury or the nobles.

Shaftesbury and the Whigs used a variety of methods to try to increase the power of their Whig Party in the 1670s. (These are described in another book in this series, *The Liberal Party*.) Newspapers, pamphlets, cartoons, plays, songs, processions, speeches—all sorts of methods were used to try to whip up support for the Whigs. But the Whigs went too far: in the Rye House Plot (1683) some of them planned to arrest the King; this failed and many of the plotters were arrested. Popular opinion swung in favour of the King and the Tories, particularly when Titus Oates was proved to be a liar who had invented the idea of the plot. Meanwhile, the King used his powers, such as taking away the rights of elections from many boroughs and amending the charters of other boroughs, so that people sympathetic to Charles would be elected.

James II and the politicians

When James II succeeded to the throne in 1685 he called for an election, which, in May of that year, produced a very friendly Parliament. In general, James was supported by the Tories and by the majority of MPs who wanted the government to go on; he was opposed by the Whigs who believed that the King's power ought to be controlled by Parliament and by law. James might have remained King for a long time if he had not tried to insist too strongly on his powers. In 1685 he tried to get Parliament to agree to the repeal of the Test Act, so that his Catholic friends could be given positions of authority in the army and in government. When they refused to do so James dismissed Parliament, which never met again. He also announced that he had the power to set aside this Test Act. A famous court case (Godden *versus* Hales) took place on this issue and the judges decided: 'There is no law that cannot be dispensed with by the lawgiver, as the laws of God may be dispensed with by God himself. . . . So likewise the law of man may be dispensed with by the legislator . . . this is not a trust granted to the King by the people but the sovereign power of the Kings of England'. If James had been allowed to get away with this there would have been no point in having a Parlia-

7 James II

ment which passed laws, nor would there have been any development of political parties—whose aim, as we have seen, is to gain control of the government.

1688 and after

This doctrine of the King's power was too much even for some Tories. They united with the Whigs and an invitation was sent to William of Orange to invade England. The overthrow of James and the accession of William and Mary (the Glorious Revolution) was followed by a series of Acts of Parliament including the Bill of Rights, the Act of Settlement and the Mutiny Act. These spelt out the wickedness of the Stuart Kings and defined the power of future British rulers. Parliament did not take from the Monarch the power to pick Ministers, to be the head of the government, or to make and carry out policy—including involving Britain in a war against France on behalf of the Dutch, although this was unpopular with the Tories in the government, with Parliament and with the country.

William and Mary's daughter, Anne, ruled from 1702 to 1714. Both Whig and Tory politicians shared in her government—the Monarch still had the power to choose Ministers, to decide policy, although the Act of Settlement insisted that there had to be elections every five years and Parliament had to meet at least at least once a year. As Bolingbroke, the Tory leader, wrote: 'We came to court . . . as all parties have done . . . to have the government of the State in our hands; our principal views were the conservation of this power, great employment to ourselves, and great opportunities of rewarding those who had helped to raise us, and of hurting those who stood in opposition to us'.

8 Queen Anne, who was a Tory by instinct but who used both Whig and Tory Ministers in her governments. Bolingbroke and other leading Tories hoped that another Stuart would succeed her—which would have required the setting aside of the Act of Settlement (1701). However, they failed to persuade even their own followers that a Catholic Stuart was preferable to a Protestant Hanoverian

9 George I, as painted by Kneller. The Elector of Hanover was the next in line of succession when Queen Anne died. His lack of interest in British affairs and his concern for the welfare of his Hanoverian territory played a large part in British political and foreign affairs after 1714

Queen Anne's death in 1714 found the Tories eager to set aside the Act of Settlement—by which the Protestant Elector of Hanover was to become King of England; they were anxious to invite a Stuart (who would have been James III) to come back as Monarch. But the Tory plot failed and George I came to the throne, determined to give office and influence to the Whigs who had remained faithful and had demanded his accession.

The Hanoverians and the Tories

The accession of George I in 1714 began a long period when the government of the country was in the hands of Whigs. If you read some of the older history books you may get the impression that everyone in Parliament was a Whig. This was not so; there were Whigs, of course, but a large number of MPs owed their position to the patronage of the Crown—and they tended to vote for whichever Minister the King had chosen. Then there was a large body of independent MPs who owed their position to no one except their own efforts—and money. Many of these were always prepared to vote for whatever government was in power, provided the government was efficient and successful. If, however, a government did something that they did not like—such as passing Walpole's Excise Bill (1733)—they used their vote to throw out the measure; if the government showed itself to be inefficient, as Whig governments did over their American policies between 1765 and 1770, then they used their power to throw out that government.

Finally, there was a small group of MPs who called themselves Tories. Some of these were the nominees of important landowners; others were independent MPs; most of them were High Anglicans who resented the growth of the power of the Nonconformists; many of them were landowners who disliked the growing influence of the merchant class with its emphasis on foreign trade and the resulting wars with France and Spain.

George III and the Tories

In 1760 George III came to the throne and used his influence to end the long domination of the Whigs. He found a pliable Minister in Lord North (1770-82) whose government finally fell when the Tories, the independent country gentlemen MPs, and some Whigs united because they were dissatisfied with the government's foolish policy towards the American colonies. The small number of Tories supported George III's attempts to end the period of Whig domination; they hoped that this might lead to their being given a share in government. In 1783 George III appointed the Younger Pitt as Chief Minister. He had served in the Whig government in 1782 which had been overthrown by the Fox-North Coalition, which in turn had been defeated over the India Bill in December 1783.

Pitt's appointment was another indication both of the King's power to pick his Ministers as he willed and his determination not to pick Whigs of the old school if he could help it. Fox and his Whig supporters sneered at the appointment of 'a schoolboy Prime Minister' in December 1783; they called his government 'the mincepie administration' which they believed they would vote out of office following the Christmas holiday. But although Pitt was defeated in vote after vote early in 1784, he remained in office; the King used his influence to persuade MPs to side with Pitt and the government and give up their support for Fox

10 William Pitt, the Younger. He became Prime Minister in 1783 when he was only twenty-four years old. Opposition to his accession was led by Fox who was supported by most leading Whigs. Although Pitt was a Whig as his father had been, Fox's opposition gave the impression that Pitt was a Tory, so Pitt's successors—Addington, Perceval, Liverpool and others —all called themselves Tories. In one sense Pitt was unconsciously the founder of the Tory Party

15

11 Respectable people had a fear of radicalism, democracy, the mob or 'the people' and their fears are illustrated in this cartoon. Reform and revolution were made to appear synonymous; reform and bloodshed were shown to be companion evils. It was cartoons such as this which encouraged support for Pitt and his Tory successors and made life difficult for Fox and the later Whigs

and the Whigs. Gradually, public opinion swung behind this government—the courage of Pitt in the face of the Opposition, his refusal to accept any of the financial rewards of office, and the influence of the King, were all factors in changing public opinion. In March 1784 Pitt asked the King to dissolve Parliament. In the following elections Pitt and the King gained a huge majority, as many of Fox's Whig supporters were defeated.

This victory did not mean that there was a Tory government in power. Pitt still called himself a Whig; he still depended on the support of the King's followers in Parliament. But it did mean that there was now a body of Whigs, followers of Fox, in Opposition to Pitt, so that gradually his government began to earn the name of 'Tory', in order to mark it off from Fox and the Whig Opposition.

The French Revolution

What finally determined the political face of the country was the onset of the French Revolution in 1789. At first most people in Britain welcomed this apparent move by the French towards constitutional government. Edmund Burke, who had first defined the roles of political parties, and had previously supported Fox and the Whigs, now wrote *Reflections on the Revolution in France*, in which he prophesied that this Revolution would end up in bloody massacres and the call for a dictator to restore society to some sort of order. Fox and his Whig followers refused to accept this teaching. Pitt and his followers became opponents of the French Revolution after 1793, by which time the revolutionaries had executed their King, invaded the Low Countries (modern Belgium and Holland), and tried to spread their revolutionary teaching throughout Europe.

In England anyone suspected of supporting the spread of the revolution was accused of being a traitor; anyone who talked about reform (of Parliament or the law) was accused of being a revolutionary in disguise; laws were brought in which allowed the arrest of suspected persons, their imprisonment without trial if need be. Judges were persuaded to give heavy penalties to people tried for spreading reforming ideas.

Fox, and a small number of Whigs, opposed this reactionary development which was, however, supported by the mass of the ruling class and by the people as a whole. Most Whigs retired from political life, leaving the ground clear for Pitt and his followers. Pitt never called himself a Tory, but many of the former Whigs, many of the King's followers, and others who supported him, did use that name. This is why in the history books the Ministries which governed Britain after Pitt's death (1806) are called Tory Ministries.

Tory principles in practice

The Tories had been hounded out of office in 1714 but by 1814 they were securely in power again. As we shall see in Chapter 2, they remained in power until 1830. This was the Party which remained true to the belief that the King had the right to govern freely—unlike Fox and his Whigs, who believed that the power of the King should be limited. The Tories also believed that the landed aristocracy were the people best suited to help the King to govern—unlike Fox and the Whigs who thought that some of the richer merchant class should be allowed a share in the governmental system. The Tories also showed their belief in 'law and order' by the legislation they passed against public meetings, demonstrations and trade unions. They feared change which they equated with revolution.

In 1714 there were some Whig MPs, some Tory MPs and many independent MPs. By 1814 this was no longer true; an increasing number of MPs had accepted a party label—although they wore it loosely, being prepared to throw away one and put on another as did Burke in the 1790s, and many of Pitt's followers in the 1800s. We will see that this looseness was a feature of British political life until the end of the nineteenth century.

Revolutionary England 1815

While George III was trying to regain the power which he thought had been taken by the Whigs, and while, later, the Younger Pitt was faced by his arch-rival, Fox, several forces were at work to change the face of Britain. The Industrial and Agricultural Revolutions were under way in the 1780s and small villages grew into towns, while towns grew into huge connurbations where 'dark satanic mills' provided work for thousands, and huge profits for the few.

The wealthy few—the industrial, professional and commercial middle class—slowly learned to live like their upper-class superiors. In large houses, with armies of servants, they lived well; their wives dressed expensively, rode in private carriages; the husbands ran their works or offices, paid their taxes and read some of the political pamphlets of the period.

12   Sheffield, one of the towns which grew as a result of the Industrial Revolution of the eighteenth and nineteenth century. Many thousands of people worked in the 'dark satanic mills'; many made their fortunes out of coal, iron and steel, railways and mills—but the unreformed Parliament almost ignored the existence of these new towns and the new wealthy, middle-class industrialists

13 An idealised and exaggerated illustration of the Peterloo Massacre, 1819, when Lancashire workmen gathered to listen to Henry Hunt (standing on the platform) at St Peter's Fields, Manchester. The Tory Government congratulated the magistrates on their decision to send in the yeomanry to disperse the crowd. But the demand for reform was too strong to be suppressed by violence such as this

And there were many such pamphlets; in the 1760s there were the writings of John Wilkes; in the 1770s there were the *Letters from Junius*, as well as Burke's *Thoughts on the Cause of the Present Discontents;* in the 1780s came the spread of the Yorkshire Association; in the 1790s Tom Paine's *Rights of Man*—and each of these was only one of many such books or organisations, all of which called for a change in the system of British government. Basically, the questions being asked were: 'Was it right that a more industrialised, urbanised Britain should be governed by a Parliament of MPs representing mainly the agricultural and under-populated areas?' 'Was it right that the rich tax–paying, economically important middle class should be excluded from a share in government?'

To confuse the issue further came the French Revolution, which so frightened the upper classes in Britain that most of them sided with Pitt's successors, who believed that revolution was the natural result of reform. They applied the old adage 'if you give them an inch they'll take a mile' to the problem of reform. The result of this attitude was a series of repressive laws: trade unions were banned, as were public meetings; newspapers were censored and a special tax imposed to make them very expensive and so less likely to be read by the poorer people. With the end of the Napoleonic Wars in 1815 came an economic depression, with thousands being thrown out of work, and millions being offered very low wages. The demonstrations by the unemployed workers alarmed the government almost as much as did illegal assemblies of the respectable working-class men who, along with middle-class radicals, campaigned for parliamentary reform. The government's answer to such demonstrations was (i) to send in the armed forces to disperse the crowds—as happened on several occasions, notably at Peterloo; (ii) to arrest real as well as imaginary leaders who might be thought capable of organising anti-government activities—as happened to Cobbett, Hunt and other radicals; (iii) to suspend *habeas corpus* so that people could be imprisoned without trial (1817); (iv) to pass a series of Six, or Gag, Acts (1819) which were intended to make it almost impossible for anti-government, pro-reform activities to get under way.

The passing of the Corn Laws

To make matters worse, the Tory government passed the Corn Laws (1815), which have been called 'the first example of naked class legislation'. During the French and Napoleonic Wars there had been a growth in population and a rise in wages; there had also been very little foreign food imported into Britain. This had enabled British farmers to charge high prices for their products—which in turn led Tory landowners to charge higher rents for their farms. All this might have come to an end in 1815 if foreign food had come into the country, so reducing prices. The passage of the Corn Laws was intended to guarantee the incomes of the landowning class. In the following year, Parliament abolished Pitt's income tax which had been imposed to help pay for the War, and replaced it with a series

14 A cartoon showing Pitt (at the Treasury) being presented with the 'promise-to-pay' bills issued by his agents at election time. In a corrupt system the government, with its control of government expenditure, found it easy to win elections

of taxes on beer, candles, sugar and the like, which further increased the cost of living for the already struggling working class.

Many of the industrial middle class had taken little interest in political affairs before 1815; the passing of the Corn Laws in the interests of the landowners drove these people out of their homes, and into the ranks of the radicals. Here they joined the workers in their demands for parliamentary reform.

We have already seen that Parliament was elected by a small number of people, most of whom were influenced by some patron—whether the Monarch or a local nobleman.

We ought not to be surprised that such a Commons passed the Corn Laws, for when a group of men gain political power they will use it for their own ends. The Corn Laws, the Gag Acts, the Game Laws, suited the landowning class which dominated the Commons and the government.

Those who resented the Corn Laws and other examples of 'naked class aggression', as well as those who hoped that parliamentary reform might lead to social, economic and legal reform, tried to make their voice heard in the period after 1815. Lord Liverpool was the Prime Minister and in his *Memoirs* he wrote about the world of 1817. He remarked that: 'They had, according to their report, proofs of a system to overthrow the constitution of the country. . . . He felt the necessity of preserving to every man his fire-side; and on these grounds he asked, for a very short time, the powers which were indispensable to the salvation of the State.'

This conviction that the demand for reform was the work of people who wanted a revolution was shared by most of Lord Liverpool's fellow-rulers.

1822 and Liberal Tories

In 1822 the Foreign Secretary, Castlereagh, committed suicide. He is recalled in a line by the radical poet, Shelley:

' I met Murder in the way—He had a mask like Castlereagh'.

The death of this prominent leader of the anti-reform movement caused Lord Liverpool to offer the post of Foreign Secretary to Canning, who was known to be slightly more liberal-minded. This annoyed some of Castlereagh's friends. Lords Eldon and Sidmouth resigned in protest, so that Liverpool was able to bring into the Cabinet other Tories, notably Peel, Huskisson and Goderich. Along with Canning, these have been called the 'Young' or 'Liberal' Tories to mark them off from their immediate reactionary predecessors.

Under Peel there took place a series of reforms affecting the legal system and prisons; under Huskisson at the Board of Trade there was a move towards lowering tariffs, including an attempt to lessen the effects of the Corn Laws without abolishing them. Trade unions were legalised, political demonstrations were allowed— and suddenly reform was respectable. After all, it was being carried out by Tories. Although Canning was Foreign Secretary he was regarded as the leader of these Liberal Tories and on Liverpool's death in 1827 he became Prime Minister.

Here we have an example of one of the reasons for the continued existence of the

15 William Huskisson, one of the 'Liberal' or 'Young' Tories who came into office in 1822. Huskisson followed the example of the Younger Pitt and lowered import and export duties as a step along the road to Free Trade. He also helped to legalise trade unions (1824) and was a supporter of Canning's policy for Catholic Emancipation. He quarrelled with the Duke of Wellington who refused to follow Canning's policy. Huskisson resigned from the Tory government and was followed by a number of young Tories—notably William Lamb (Lord Melbourne) and Lord Palmerston. Although he was killed at the opening of the Liverpool railway in 1830, his followers gained prominence in the Whig government which came into office in that year

Tory Party: it is quite prepared to change its policies when popularity demands it, and has not been hampered by philosophies, fixed policies, or pre-determined constitutions. It has had the capacity to deal with issues as they arose; to behave in what is nowadays called a pragmatic fashion.

Religion and the fall of the Tories

Canning was known to be opposed to parliamentary reform; he agreed with his former leader, Lord Liverpool, who had once said: 'We must all be agreed that the House of Commons is a legislative body. . . . He supposed every person would agree that the landed interest ought to have the preponderant weight. The landed interest was, in fact, the stamina of the country. . . .'

But Canning was known to be in favour of religious toleration which required the repeal of the Test Acts (Chapter I), which prevented Nonconformists—including Catholics—from enjoying the civil liberty enjoyed by Anglicans. It is likely that, had he lived, Canning would have proposed such a repeal. Unfortunately, Canning died and after a short ministry under Goderich, Wellington became Prime Minister, with Robert Peel as the leader of the House of Commons. Neither of these was in favour of any move towards appeasing the Catholics. Both of them were influenced by their experiences of Catholic Ireland—where Wellington had lived and where Peel, as Chief Secretary, had earned the nickname of 'Orange' Peel because of the way he supported the ruling Protestant group. Because of this attitude, several of Canning's supporters refused to serve in Wellington's government—notably Huskisson, Palmerston and William Lamb (Lord Melbourne).

It was from Ireland that the challenge to Wellington's government came—not the last time that a Tory government would face Irish problems. Daniel O'Connell, a Catholic lawyer, organised a Catholic Association with the aim of achieving Home Rule for Ireland. Since Home Rule would have to be passed through the British House of Commons, O'Connell began a campaign for Catholic Emancipation (or freedom) so that Catholics could be eligible to become MPs. O'Connell's campaign is interesting since it was the first successful campaign to form a political party led by people outside Parliament; the other parties had been formed by MPs to gain support for their ideas. It is also interesting because it was a well-organised movement, using the Catholic churches in villages and towns as centres for recruiting support and collecting money; in this it was of some use to the later Anti-Corn Law League which appreciated the value of constituency organisation.

O'Connell decided to challenge the government by offering himself as a candidate in a by-election in County Clare in 1828. The result was a sweeping victory for O'Connell, the growth of support for his movement and the increased danger of a Catholic rising. At first Wellington and Peel wanted to obey the law as it stood

16 Canning addressing his constituents at Liverpool in 1812. He was the leader of the Young Tories in 1822 and became Prime Minister in succession to Liverpool in 1827. Unfortunately he died within a year of taking office and his 'liberal' supporters were excluded from office by the die-hard Wellington who became Prime Minister in 1828

THE FIELD OF BATTERSEA

17 This caricature records the duel fought between Wellington and the Earl of Winchelsea who had accused Wellington of dishonesty because of the change in policy over Catholic Emancipation. The duel, in which neither party was injured, took place on 21 March 1829

and refuse O'Connell permission to take his seat in the Commons. But, as Peel himself wrote at the time: 'The events of the Clare election, with the conviction that the same scenes would be enacted in nearly every county in Ireland, if matters were to remain just as they have been for the last five or six years, convinced me that it was not safe for the Protestant interest in Ireland that they should remain so. . . .'

But it was not as simple as that. Lord Eldon and the old Tories were unwilling to accept this proposed change; George IV was opposed to it, as was the Anglican Church. Peel wrote:

> The chief difficulty was with the King. . . . To Lord Eldon he had said, 'that if he gave assent to the Roman Catholic Relief Bill, he would go to the Baths abroad, to Hanover; that he would return no more to England, and that his subjects might get a Catholic King in the Duke of Clarence' . . . I now feared that the difficulties were almost insuperable. There was the declared opinion of the King, the declared opinion of the House of Lords, the declared opinion of the Church, unfavourable to the measures we were disposed to recommend. Being convinced that the Catholic question must be settled . . . I determined not to insist upon retirement from office, but to make the Duke the voluntary offer of official co-operation.

PARTIAL DISTRESS,
Or the Old CABINET - MAKER and his Man out of Employment.

18 Wellington and Peel are shown as unemployed carpenters. In February 1830 the King's speech had referred to the 'partial distress' of the agricultural workers; the word 'partial' had caused great bitterness, particularly among the unemployed and lowly paid—and their radical sympathisers. When Wellington's government was defeated in November 1830, the Duke resigned—and so became one of the 'unemployed'. Both Peel and Wellington were very rich men and their 'partial distress' was unlike that of the poor

Here we have illustrated several of the features of the Tory Party; it is reluctant to make a reform—unlike more radical parties which have introduced most of the changes that have improved our society. It is, however, always willing to bow to pressure and accept the need for a reform if the pressure is great enough. Peel, who had so vigorously opposed Canning's proposals for Emancipation was willing—although reluctant—to introduce that measure himself. Finally, we see the right wing of the Party (under Lord Eldon) remaining obstinate to the last, refusing to change its mind. The Tory Party has always had these 'last ditchers', even in the twentieth century.

Tories out

In 1830 the old Tories got their own back on the renegade Wellington by voting him out of office, which allowed Grey and the Whigs to come in. In the ensuing election the old Tories used their influence to prevent the election of Tories who were known to be followers of Wellington and Peel—which helped the Whigs to a majority in the Commons and so paved the way for the Reform Act of 1832.

It is often claimed that Peel showed great strength of character in being willing to put the national interest before Party policy by preferring to change his mind rather than risk a Civil War in Ireland. Later on we shall see him do the same over the Corn Laws (Chapter 3). Disraeli, another future Tory leader (Chapter 4), did not approve of Peel's inconsistencies. Speaking in 1846, he said:

I remember him making his Protection speeches. . . . It was a great thing to hear the Right Hon gentleman say : 'I would rather be the leader of the gentlemen

19 A contemporary view of 'Public determination driving the Tories out of office in 1830'

of England than possess the confidence of sovereigns'. That was a grand thing. We don't hear much of the 'gentlemen of England' now. . . . Protection appears to be in about the same condition that Protestantism was in 1828. The country will draw its moral. . . . He has tampered with the generous confidence of a great people and a great party. . . . For me there remains this at least—the opportunity of expressing thus publicly my belief that a Conservative government is an organised hypocrisy.

But, as we shall see, Disraeli's own career was riddled with similar inconsistencies which seem to be part of the make-up of a Tory leader.

3   Peel and Conservatism, 1830–1850

Parliamentary reform

The 1830 election was almost a referendum, since there was only one issue which was spoken of or written about—parliamentary reform. The parliamentary system was basically the one which had been established in the Stuart period. Each county returned two MPs, while certain boroughs which had been important centres of population in the past returned the rest. We have seen that the Industrial Revolution was rapidly changing the face of Britain. But most of these new towns were unrepresented in Parliament while the Cornish village of East Looe had two MPs and so did West Looe, although their total population was not more than 3,000.

Fox and the Whigs had supported moves towards parliamentary reform in the 1770s and 1780s. Grey, Fox's successor, had supported demands for reform in the 1820s. Now that at last the Whigs were back in power it was assumed that they would 'go for reform'.

The Reform Bills

Wellington and the Tories were opposed to reform. 'The system of representation possesses the full and entire confidence of the country' said Wellington in 1830, revealing one feature of Toryism which is an unwillingness to face distasteful facts. The evident truth was that the system was opposed by the bulk of the population. In Norwich, Nottingham, Bristol, Derby, London and—above all—Birmingham, there were massive and noisy demonstrations in favour of reform. The London mob marched up Piccadilly to Apsley House where Wellington lived on the edge of Hyde Park and smashed their way through railings to demonstrate their support for reform.

In March 1831 Lord John Russell introduced the First Reform Bill in the Commons; it proposed the abolition of a number of rotten boroughs and the redistribution of the seats to some of the industrial towns. Many of those listening realised for the first time what reform would mean—they would lose their influence over elections, some of them would lose their place in the Commons and the chance to make profitable pickings. When a vote was taken on this First Bill, Macaulay the historian was in the Commons as a Whig supporter of reform. He wrote to a friend, T. F. Ellis, on 30 March 1831:

> Such a scene as the division of last Tuesday I never saw, and never expect to see again. . . . The crowd overflowed the House in every part. When the strangers were cleared out, and the doors locked, we had six hundred and eight members

20 Sir Robert Peel, Senior (1750–1830), was responsible as an MP for the Factory Acts passed in 1802 and 1819. He was the father of Sir Robert Peel (*Picture* 24) the 'young' Tory who first opposed Canning's policy on Catholic Emancipation, then changed his mind in 1829. This reversal of policy helped to split the Tory Party and let the Whigs in. As Prime Minister, Peel continued the work of Huskisson for Free Trade, and influenced by Cobden (*Picture* 23), repealed the Corn Laws which once again split the Party

21 The seventh Earl of Shaftesbury, Ashley Cooper. The first Earl had founded the Whig Party in the seventeenth century. The seventh Earl was a Tory best remembered for his work for factory reform.

present. . . . The Ayes and Noes were like two volleys of cannon from opposite sides of a field of battle. When the Opposition went out into the lobby . . . we spread ourselves over the benches on both sides of the House: . . . when the doors were shut we began to speculate on our numbers. Everybody was desponding. We have lost it. We are only two hundred and eighty at the most. . . . They are three hundred. . . . We were all standing up and stretching forward, telling with the tellers. At three hundred there was a short cry of joy—at three hundred and two another—suppressed however in a moment: for we did not yet know what the hostile force might be.

The doors were thrown open and in they came. Each of them, as he entered, brought some different report of their numbers. . . . Alexander Barry told me that he had counted, and that they were three hundred and four. We were all breathless with anxiety, when Charles Wood, who stood near the door, jumped on a bench and cried out: 'They are only three hundred and one'. We sent up a shout that you might have heard to Charing Cross, waving our hats, stamping against the floor, and clapping our hands. The tellers scarcely got through the floor. . . . But you might have heard a pin drop as Duncannon read the numbers. Then again the shouts broke out, and many of us shed tears. And the jaw of Peel fell, and the face of Twiss was as the face of a damned soul; and Herries looked like Judas taking his necktie off for the final operation.

But Macaulay's rejoicing was short-lived because the Bill was defeated in the Committee stage in the Commons. In the ensuing election the Whigs gained a majority—the popular demand for reform being reflected in the number of patrons who 'influenced' the return of MPs willing to support Grey. The Bill then went through the Commons safely, only to be rejected by the Lords where Wellington and the Tories were in a majority. This was the cause of even more demonstration and rioting during which the centre of Bristol was burnt to the ground, as was Nottingham Castle. Grey rushed another Bill through the Commons and this time the Lords merely attempted to amend the Bill—not reject it. Grey asked King William to create fifty new Peers so that he could get the Bill through the Lords. William, anxious to stave off reform and eager to placate his friends in the Lords, refused to do so. Grey therefore resigned and William asked Wellington to form a government.

For a week Wellington tried to do so; Peel and other Tories were not willing to support him. In *Coningsby* Disraeli wrote: 'On the 15th [May] all was over . . . after five days' exertion, this man of indomitable will and invincible fortunes, resigns the task in discomfiture and despair. . . . From that moment power passed from the House of Lords to another assembly.'

The King was forced to ask Grey to become Prime Minister again, to promise to create fifty Peers if this proved necessary, and to use his influence with the Lords to get them to allow the Reform Bill through. In June 1832 the Third Reform Bill was finally passed; as Disraeli noted this was the beginning of the end of the power of the Lords.

22 Woman dragging coal—part of the evidence presented to the Royal Commission on conditions in the mines (1840–41). Liberals believed that government had no part to play in the nation's economic and social life. Tories believed that the government had to protect those who were unable to protect themselves

Tories and reform

In 1832 the Reform Act passed into law and fifty-six rotten boroughs with populations of under 2,000 lost their right to have MPs, while thirty-one others were deprived of one seat but allowed to retain one. The seats available were then distributed:

1. *Gaining two seats:* Manchester, Birmingham, Leeds, Greenwich, Sheffield, Sunderland, Devonport, Wolverhampton, Tower Hamlets, Finsbury, Mary-le-Bone, Lambeth, Bolton, Bradford, Brighton, Halifax, Macclesfield, Oldham, Stockport, Stoke-on-Trent, Stroud.

2. *Gaining one seat:* Ashton-under-Lyne, Bury, Chatham, Cheltenham, Dudley, Frome, Gateshead, Huddersfield, Kidderminster, Kendal, Rochdale, Salford, South Shields, Tynemouth, Wakefield, Walsall, Warrington, Whitby, Whitehaven, Merthyr Tydfil.

The vote was given to the £10 householder. If we translate that into a modern equivalent it would include any man who owned a property of which the rateable value was £800 a year—which explains why only about 250,000 got the vote in 1832. Only the rich, middle class gained from this Act, as *The Poor Man's Guardian* explained in December 1832: 'We have often told you the Reform Bill would do you no good. . . . The great majority of the new electors are middlemen who thrive by your degradation'.

The new Parliament did not look very different from the old; over half the MPs were elected in agricultural constituencies; 500 of the 658 MPs were still connected with the landed gentry, 217 being the sons of members of the House of Lords.

The landed gentry realised that they had been attacked by the Whigs and that the Reform Act was a concession to the growing power of industrialists. This was one reason for factory reform being taken up by Tories such as Lord Shaftesbury—the descendant of the leader of the first Whig Party. Aided by fellow Tories and the Whig landed gentry, he persuaded Parliament to pass the first effective Factory Act in 1833, and continued to press for further factory reform throughout his life. However, the Tory interest in reform was not entirely due to a desire to take revenge on their upstart rivals. As Disraeli recalled in a speech in 1843, the landowning class—unlike the industrial middle class (or 'Cottontots' of Manchester), who were driven only by the selfish desire for personal gain—had always been aware of their duty: 'I have heard from Mr Cobden . . . that England was the victim of the feudal system. . . . I regret that not more of it is remaining . . . the principle of the feudal system is that the tenure of all property should be the performance of its duties'.

Peel and modern Conservatism

For four months at the end of 1834, Peel was Prime Minister. In January 1835 there was a general election during which Peel issued a statement to his constituents at Tamworth. This Manifesto, as it has been called, is important because it showed that Peel, at least, had accepted the 1832 Reform Act, that he acknowledged the need for more moderate reform and so was asking for support from the new middle classes for his Conservatism: 'The spirit of the Reform Bill implies a careful review of institutions, civil and ecclesiastical, undertaken in a friendly temper, combining, with the firm maintenance of established rights, the correction of proved abuses and the redress of real grievances—in that case, I can for myself and colleagues undertake to act in such a spirit and with such intentions'.

Disraeli and Peel

Disraeli, the son of a Jewish country gentleman, had been baptised a Christian in the hope that this would make his life an easier one. By 1835 Disraeli had worked out his own political ideas, based on the theory that before the Industrial Revolution there had been a 'good' society in which the landed gentry governed and looked after the people. Their replacement by the profit-seeking middle class was something he deplored. In a novel, *Coningsby*, he attacked Peel's Conservatism as outlined in the Tamworth Manifesto: '. . . millions are accumulated . . . evidence exists of a state of demoralisation in the once happy population of this land, which is not equalled in the most barbarous countries. . . . I cannot help suspecting that this has arisen because property has been permitted to be created and held without the performance of its duties'.

Peel led the Conservatives to victory in the 1841 election. He inherited a financial and trade muddle from the Melbourne (Whig) government, which he set about putting right. Tariffs on raw materials and manufactured goods were lowered, prices fell, demand for goods increased. There was a rise in employment

23 Richard Cobden, a successful industrialist, was one of the founders of the Anti-Corn Law League (1838) which succeeded in getting these laws repealed in 1846. Cobden and his followers became very rich reaping the harvest of the Industrial Revolution in Victorian Britain. They were opposed to government interference in the nation's economic and social life—so they were opposed to tariffs as well as Factory Acts

and in profits. Peel also carried out a series of reforms which strengthened the country's banking system and so helped the industrial middle classes. To appease the humanitarian Tories, led by Shaftesbury, he passed a number of Factory and Mines Acts which made life easier for the working classes.

This was efficient and successful government, but, asked Disraeli, was it Tory government? Was there any difference between this government and one that might be led by one of the new MPs from the manufacturing towns? The final break with Peel came over the issue of the Corn Laws. These, as we have seen, had been imposed by a Tory Parliament in 1815. In 1838 an Anti-Corn Law League had been set up by merchants and manufacturers from the industrial areas, with its headquarters in Manchester. Some of its leaders—notably Cobden and Bright, were elected to Parliament. Peel realised that he led the party of the country gentlemen whose interests required the Corn Laws to protect them from foreign competition. But Cobden and others argued that if industrialists were not to be protected there was no logical reason for protecting landed gentry; if cotton was to be exposed to foreign competition, then so should corn be exposed; if Free Trade was good for one commodity, it was good for all.

Throughout 1842–5 Peel defended himself against these attacks from the Cobdenite wing of the Whig Opposition. But the force of Cobden's arguments added to the onset of the Irish famine combined to make Peel change his mind about the Corn Laws, as he had done about Emancipation (Chapter 2). As he said in a speech in the Commons in February 1846: 'I admit that a natural consequence of the course I have pursued is to alienate a great party. . . . I know what would have conciliated temporary confidence. . . . It would have been to underrate the danger in Ireland, to invite a united combination for the maintenance of the existing Corn Law . . . by such a course I should have been sure to animate and please a party.'

Disraeli regarded this as the great betrayal. As he said in the same debate:

The agricultural interest is that great body of people who are the cultivators of the earth; and if you materially change the balance between the populations that depend upon the two great interests of this country, you shake to its centre that territorial constitution, you destroy the security for local government, you subvert the guarantee for public liberty; you change, in fact, the character of England; you bring about the social revolution which the Right Hon gentleman always reminded us would be the consequence of following the policy of the school of Manchester.

Tories out

Disraeli led a small band of country gentlemen in opposition to Peel, who was followed by all the leading lights of the Party—Aberdeen, Gladstone and others who later joined with the Whigs to form the Liberal Party of the 1860s. For Disraeli there seemed a poor future. How was a Tory with his ideas about the aristocracy, the industrial middle class, to make his mark in British politics?

24 Peel addressing the Commons in 1846 while introducing his motion for the repeal of the Corn Laws. Facing him are the Whigs, including Cobden and Bright, the leaders of the Anti-Corn Law League. Behind Peel are the Tories. The majority, including all the leaders and eminent men, followed Peel and supported his Free Trade policy. In the 1850s these Peelites joined with the Whigs to give birth to the Liberal Party, which took office under a former Peelite, William Ewart Gladstone. The small number of backbenchers who opposed Peel followed Lord George Bentinck and a young novelist, Benjamin Disraeli

33

That he did so is a tribute to the man. Peel is sometimes called the father of modern Conservatism; in the sense that he was willing to change his mind, to recognise the need for change in an England that was no longer an agricultural country, all this may support his claim. But his attempts foundered in 1846 when the Corn Laws were repealed and his Party split and were driven from office. 1832 was a political victory for the new middle class; 1846 was their economic triumph; England, it seemed, belonged to them.

4 Changing Fortunes of the Tory Party

In 1846, as we have seen, the Tory—or Conservative—Party was split over the Corn Laws. The Peelite wing joined the Whigs and with them formed the Liberal Party. The small band of followers who supported Disraeli were unknown back-benchers, the country gentlemen. For the next thirty years, Parliament was dominated by the Whigs led by Russell, Gladstone and Palmerston. The Tories held office for only three brief periods during this time, and it was during the second of these that the Second Reform Act of 1867 was passed. Although Disraeli became Prime Minister in 1868 when Derby retired, and was delighted that he had climbed to the top of the 'greasy pole' of politics, his Party lost the election of 1868 and let in Gladstone and the first recognisably Liberal government, which lasted until 1874.

However, in the thirty years after this (1874–1906) they were in office for most of the time; the Liberals held office only in 1880–86 and again in 1892–5. The party which had been excluded from office for almost thirty years became the party which held office almost continually. This remarkable turnround in the fortunes of the Tory Party is due, very largely, to Disraeli, who had helped to split the Party in 1846. He, more than any other politician, deserves the title 'founder of the Party'.

Disraeli and class

Although Disraeli was the son of a Jewish immigrant he became, like many immigrants, more English than the English. In 1836 he wrote:

> England has become great by her institutions. Her hereditary Crown has insured us from the evils of a contested succession; her Peerage, interested . . . in the good government of the country, has offered a . . . bulwark against the violence of popular passion; her House of Commons . . . has enlisted the mass of the lesser proprietors of the country in favour of a political system; . . . her ecclesiastical establishment . . . has maintained the sacred cause of learning and religion, and . . . secured toleration.

We will see later this insistence on the importance of the Monarchy, the Lords, the country gentlemen and the Church. What is also significant is Disraeli's failure to mention the middle class as being of much importance. He thought that this class was a selfish one with little sense of responsibility to the rest of the community. In 1848 he said: 'the gentlemen opposite to me are a middle-class

25 Queen Victoria visiting Disraeli, December 1877. Here they can be seen at the Railway Station, High Wycombe. Under Disraeli's influence the Tory Party 'adopted' the monarchy while the Queen repaid the Party by favouring Disraeli and showing her dislike for Gladstone, the Liberal leader. This link between the Party and the monarchy has remained a feature of British political life

government—they look to the middle class for power, and the middle class look to them for their advantage ... that we have the arrogant authority of a class who obtained power by false pretences, and now, possessing it, attempt to exercise it merely for their own advantage'.

The middle class was a town class—unlike, Disraeli's Tory country gentlemen. This middle class of industrialists had been responsible for the creation of Britain's towns which Disraeli wrote about in his novel *Sybil* in 1845: 'In great cities men are brought together by the desire of gain ... they are careless of neighbours. Christianity teaches us to love our neighbours as oneself; modern society acknowledges no neighbour'.

The Tories and the monarch

After the death of Prince Albert, Queen Victoria had gone into a long period of mourning, earning for herself the nickname 'the widow of Windsor'. It was left to Disraeli to persuade the Queen to come out of her retirement and take her place in the world again. In 1876 he persuaded Parliament to give her the title 'Empress of India'; his daily reports to the Queen of parliamentary business assumed almost the role of romantic letters. On her side the Queen showed her

36

THE CHOICE OF HERCULES.

26 Disraeli (right) inviting John Bull (centre) to follow the empire-building path while Gladstone (left) points to another path. John Bull—and the British electorate—preferred the Tory path of expansion and glory

approval of Disraeli—who was allowed to sit in her presence whereas Gladstone had to kneel or stand.

This seems to be unimportant. In fact, as the Queen got older she became universally more popular; her Jubilees of 1887 and 1897 were occasions of national and international rejoicing. Her popularity flowed over onto the Tory Party, which had adopted her, so that many people assumed that she was almost a paid-up member, if not leader, of that Party. 'For Queen and Country' could easily become for 'Queen and Party' in the minds of the less-sophisticated electorate.

The Tories and Empire

Disraeli had once described the colonies as 'millstones round the neck of England' which had to pay for their defence, get involved in foreign wars to prevent a take-over by other foreign powers and which could expect that the colonies would one day break their ties with this country (as the Americans had done). However, in the 1870s Disraeli changed his attitude. He became conscious of the growth of Imperialism—the desire by European powers for ever-increasing stretches of territory in overseas countries. This movement had a short life; by 1914 it was already on the wane. But while it lasted it was a powerful movement and one which Disraeli captured for the Tories.

Popular support for this policy of British expansion was reflected in the music hall song of 1877:

We don't want to fight
But by Jingo, if we do,
We've got the ships
We've got the men
We've got the money too!

Tory foreign policy

It was Disraeli who coined the phrase 'patriotism is the last refuge of the scoundrel'. But as a practical politician as well as a convert to Englishness, Disraeli appreciated the popularity of Lord Palmerston who seemed to treat the rest of the world as if it were a British preserve. When Palmerston died in 1865 the emerging Liberal Party with its policies of peace, negotiations, respect for the opinions of foreign powers, created a vacuum into which Disraeli led his Tories. They took over the mantle of Palmerston and they, not Palmerston's Liberal successors, became the 'patriotic party'.

Lord Salisbury, leader of the Party, wrote on Disraeli's death in 1881:

His feelings . . . with respect to the greatness of his country . . . made an impression on his countrymen. Zeal for the greatness of England was the passion of his life . . . the people recognised the force with which this desire dominated his actions, and they repaid it by an affection . . . which did not depend on . . . opinions as to the particular policy pursued. This was his great title to their attachment, that above all things he wished to see England united, and powerful, and great.

Tories and social reform

Disraeli attacked the middle classes for having power without responsibility, whereas he believed that the landed gentry had always used their power in the interests of those over whom they were set. This helps to explain his concern for social progress. If Britain's cities were squalid places this was because the middle class had made them so. Tory government would make these places more fit for people to live in. As he said in 1872:

I ventured to say a short time ago, speaking in one of the great cities of this country, that the health of the people was the most important question for a statesman. . . . It involves the state of the dwellings of the people. . . . It involves their enjoyment of air, light and water. . . . It involves the purity of their provisions. . . . What is the opinion of the great Liberal Party on this subject? A leading member . . . denounced them the other day as a 'policy of sewage'. Well, it may be a 'policy of sewage' to a Liberal. . . . But to one of the labouring multitude of England, who has found fever to be one of the members of his household . . . it is not a 'policy of sewage', but a question of life and death . . . is it all that wonderful that they should wish to elevate and improve their condition, and it is unreasonable that they should ask the legislature to assist them . . . as far as it is consistent with the general welfare of the realm?

27 Disraeli (seated left) with some of the members of his Cabinet, 1878. From left to right: Earl Derby (the 'uncrowned King of Lancashire') Lord Cairns, Sir Stafford Northcote (later Lord Iddlesleigh), Disraeli, Gathorne Hardy, and the Marquis of Salisbury—Disraeli's successor

He was true to his word. His government (1874–80) passed two Housing Acts (1875 and 1879) which were the first serious attempts to organise slum clearance; there was a Public Health Act (1875) which laid down the guide lines for reforming efforts well into the present century. There was the first Food and Drugs Act to ensure that shops were healthier places and the Sandow Act which went a long way to making elementary education compulsory; a Trade Union Act which legalised picketing, a Factory Act which at last brought in the ten–hour day, and the Merchant Shipping Act which compelled ships to have the Plimsoll Line as one means of making ships safer.

This policy was attacked by the Liberals, with their belief in *laissez faire* or non-interference; it was, however, welcomed by the radicals, led by Chamberlain who—as Mayor of Birmingham—took advantage of Disraeli's legislation to transform Birmingham by slum clearance and provide libraries, parks, baths and other amenities. It was also welcomed by many working-class leaders. Alexander Macdonald was the first working man to be elected to Parliament. He said that Disraeli had done more for the working man in six years than the Liberals had done in fifty.

Tories and the working classes
Disraeli believed that the upper classes had some sort of divine right to govern— provided that they did so in the interests of the people as a whole. He was not a democrat in the modern sense; he did not believe that the people should share in

39

the electoral system. In 1836 he wrote: 'I deny that a people can govern itself . . . power must be exercised by a minority of numbers. . . . The phrase "the people" is sheer nonsense'.

But in 1867 he introduced the Second Reform Act which gave the vote to all householders and to lodgers paying at least £10 a year in rent in the boroughs, although in the counties the vote was not substantially changed. Disraeli delightedly said that he has 'dished the Whigs' by this Act: he had, after all, led the opposition to a much milder Reform Bill in 1866, when he said: 'The moment you have universal suffrage . . . you will have a horde of selfish and obscure mediocrities. . . . I think that this House should remain a House of Commons, and not become a House of the People'.

But popular opinion was evidently in favour of reform; when the gates of Hyde Park were closed to try to stop a reform meeting, the crowd simply pushed the railings down. In the face of such popular clamour Disraeli gave way, hoping to cash in on the popularity which he thought would follow. Sir John Gorst, Conservative Party agent from 1870 to 1877 wrote: 'The people may be trusted to use electoral power to . . . support those who are promoting their interests'. The Tories hoped that the working-class voters would ally with their upper-class rulers to keep the middle classes out of power.

Toryism 1880

Disraeli was defeated in the election of 1880 and retired from political life. He had struggled since 1846, first to show his small band of country gentlemen what they should believe in, and then to show the country as a whole that Toryism was worth supporting. His success was reflected in the long period of Tory rule from 1886 onwards.

His Imperialism, jingoism and social reforms attracted the support of the working class. The upper classes supported him because he guaranteed them a place in the sun. Many former Liberals supported him because they believed his policies were more British than were the policies put forward by Gladstone.

By 1880 the Tory Party had been identified as the party of Empire, Crown and active foreign policy, led by the upper classes. It has retained many of these allegiancies.

5   Salisbury and Conservatism, 1880-1900

Party organisation

The Conservative Party does not consist only of three hundred or so MPs and some members of the House of Lords. These are the ones we see on TV, hear about on the radio or read about in the newspapers. But the Party is much larger than its parliamentary representatives. Each constituency in the country is divided into electoral wards and in each ward the Party has an organisation with a chairman, secretary and treasurer; the wards send representatives to the constituency organisation which in turn sends delegates to regional and national organisations. This means that many thousands of people are involved in the affairs of the Party who never get into the news.

All this was unnecessary in the days of the unreformed Parliament when elections were often decided on local, and not national issues and when the local patron would make sure that people knew why they should vote for a particular candidate.

But after the Reform Act of 1832 things had to change. There was an increase in the number of the electors, so that the old methods of controlling elections would no longer do. It was essential that the Party ensured that its supporters got their names put on to the Register of Electors. If they neglected to do so they would not be able to vote. Local Associations were formed to supervise the registering of electors. To co-ordinate the work of these local Associations the Tory Party set up a national headquarters at the Carlton Club in London—a Club to which every Tory MP had to belong.

The question of organisation became even more important when the 1867 Act gave the vote to the skilled workers and the 1872 Ballot Act lessened the influence which a patron might have over the voters. In November 1867 representatives of fifty-five constituencies met in the Freemasons' Tavern, London, under the chairmanship of John Gorst, MP, to 'consider by what organisation we may make Conservative principles effective among the masses'. They formed the National Union of Conservative and Constitutional Associations. Every local Conservative Association could join the Union by paying one guinea (£1.05) per year. The functions of the Union were outlined by H. Cecil Raikes, Chairman from 1869 to 1874, who said: 'any party who wished to retain their hold upon the country must ascertain how far their proceedings were in harmony with the wishes of the people'.

Following his defeat in the 1868 election, Disraeli established the Conservative Central office to act as a centre for the Party's funds, to prepare election propaganda for the Party's candidates and to prepare pamphlets and notes which could

29 The dominant figure of the Marquis of Salisbury who was Prime Minister 1886–1892 and 1895–1902. This aristocrat had resigned from Disraeli's Cabinet in 1867 rather than agree to the Second Reform Act. His distaste for reform was also shown by his opposition to the reforming zeal of Randolph Churchill

28 Lord Randolph Churchill. Between 1880 and 1885 Churchill led a small group of Conservative MPs in their continual opposition to Gladstone's Liberal government. This group became known as the Fourth Party

be used by MPs in the Commons and by candidates in the constituencies. In 1872 the National Union of Conservative Associations moved its headquarters into the same building in which the Central Office was already established. Here was the 'nuts and bolts' centre of the Party, although the leaders continued to make their headquarters at the Carlton Club.

Lord Randolph Churchill
Churchill, the third son of the Duke of Marlborough, first attracted public attention by his attacks on Gladstone in the 1880s. He stood out as the political heir to Disraeli with his belief in Tory democracy and his slogan 'trust the people'. He soon made himself spokesman for the National Union. He demanded that this Union should become more representative, by allowing a greater number of working men to become active members; he also asked that the Union should be given more power to decide Party policy. This was not regarded with much enthusiasm by Salisbury, who distrusted the people.

In 1886 Salisbury became Prime Minister and he gave Churchill the important post of Chancellor of the Exchequer. There were 316 Tory MPs plus the 78 Liberal Unionists who had split with Gladstone over the question of Home Rule for Ireland; the Liberals had only 191 MPs. This put Salisbury in a strong position; he was able to ignore the radical wing of the Party led by Churchill. In December 1886 Churchill wanted the Cabinet to reduce the military estimates for the following

42

year. When he could not get his way, he wrote a letter of resignation. He thought he was indispensable—as a leader in the Commons and as a popular figure outside. But Salisbury accepted the resignation—and Churchill's career came to a sudden end. With his departure the Tory Party tended to forget Disraeli's ideas on Tory democracy and social development, at least for the time being.

The changing nature of the Party, 1886

Salisbury was in a strong position in 1886, largely as the result of the break-up of the Liberal Party. One section of old Whigs, led by Lord Hartington, had decided to leave the Liberals because they thought that after the passing of the Third Reform Act (1884–5) Gladstone would become too radical. On the other hand, the radical Liberals, led by Joseph Chamberlain, left Gladstone because they thought he would not be radical enough and the gulf was widened over the Irish Home Rule issue. Chamberlain believed that it was his radical campaign which had helped the Liberals to win many seats in working-class areas; if Gladstone was going to spend his time, and Parliament's, on an Irish Home Rule Bill then there would not be time for the passage of the social legislation that Chamberlain wanted. So the Liberals broke up—in Parliament the dissidents tended to vote with the Tories while in the country many former Liberal supporters became Tory voters.

This is one explanation of the Tory behaviour towards the lower classes in the next twenty years. They ignored social problems such as poverty, even when

30 The Irish Party, which, under Parnell, exercised such an important influence on the fortunes of the Tory and Liberal Parties in the late nineteenth century

31 A painting of some of those homeless who lived on London's streets in Victorian and Edwardian England. Liberal retrenchment with its emphasis on low taxation, and Tory imperialism with its attention turned overseas ignored these less well-off members of society

these were brought to public notice. In 1900, Rowntree, the social reformer, discovered that about one-third of the population lived in a state of poverty. He defined this in the following way:

> . . . in which the total family earnings were insufficient to obtain the minimum necessities for the maintenance of even physical efficiency. . . . And let us clearly understand what 'merely physical efficiency' means. A family living upon the scale allowed for in this estimate must never spend a penny on railway or omnibus; never go into the country unless they walk; never purchase a half-penny newspaper or buy a ticket for a popular concert; never write letters to absent children, for they cannot afford the postage. They cannot save, join sick club or trade union; they cannot pay the subscriptions. The children have no pocket money for dolls, marbles or sweets. The father must not smoke or drink. The mother must never buy any pretty clothes for herself or for her children. (*'Poverty, a study of Town Life', Rowntree, 1900*).

The Tory government seemed to go out of their way to make life even more difficult for the working class. In July 1901, the House of Lords issued their decision in the Taff Vale case. A railway union in South Wales had gone on strike against increased working hours and less pay and the owners of the railway then sued the union for damages. The Law Lords came out against the union and ordered them to pay £19,000 damages plus £23,000 costs. This decision, at the time, looked likely to bring about the end of all union power.

The Tory government could have passed an Act to set aside the legal decision,

44

but it was left to the Liberals to do it by the Trade Disputes Act 1906. The Tories, under Salisbury until 1902, then under his nephew, Balfour, had forgotten their Tory democracy and seemed to have become an anti-working-class party under the influence of the Liberal element which had crept in after 1886.

Imperialism by private enterprise

One feature of Tory democracy which the Salisbury Tories did not forget was imperialism. The government gave active support to a number of private companies which set out to gain control of various parts of Africa. Between 1884 and 1892, over 350 Nigerian chiefs made treaties with the Royal Niger Company which gradually took over what is now called Nigeria. In 1889 the Colonial Secretary wrote to Lord Salisbury who doubled as Prime Minister and Foreign Secretary:

> *Sir*, I am directed by Lord Knutsford to transmit to you the correspondence between this Department and Lord Gifford, VC, Chairman of the Exploring Company (Limited) about a company to be formed for developing the Bechuanaland Protectorate and the countries to the north.

32 In 1886 and 1887 the Social Democratic Federation (one of the many Socialist societies founded in this period) led demonstrations of unemployed workmen. These often led to rioting and looting. After one such demonstration the leaders were arrested and tried at the Old Bailey. In the dock can be seen Jack Williams, H. M. Hyndman (an old Etonian Marxist), H. H. Champion and John Burns—who helped organise the London Dockers' Strike 1889, and the Labour Representation Committee 1900. He became a member of the Liberal government 1906

[I also enclose] a letter from Mr C. J. Rhodes, of the Cape Colony, and two other gentlemen, who, as representing the holders of . . . the Concession from Lo Bengula, state that they have arranged . . . to co-operate in any such scheme as that proposed. In fact, it is understood that . . . Lord Gifford and Mr Rhodes hope to be able to unite . . . all the existing British interests in the Protectorate and the countries to the northwards.

[Lord Knutsford] thinks that such a company will . . . come directly subject to control by Her Majesty's government. . . . The example of the Imperial East African Company shows that such a body may to some considerable extent relieve Her Majesty's government from diplomatic difficulties and heavy expenditure. In Lord Knutsford's judgment such a company as that proposed for the Bechuanaland Protectorate, if well conducted, would render still more valuable assistance to Her Majesty's government in South Africa.

Imperialism and unemployment

Cecil Rhodes, the founder of modern Rhodesia, believed that the British should colonise as much of the world as they could. In 1895 he wrote: 'I attended a meeting of unemployed. I listened to the wild speeches. . . . We colonial statesmen must acquire new lands for settling the surplus population, to provide new markets for the goods produced in the factories and mines. . . . If you want to avoid civil war, you must become imperialists'.

33 The entry of Buller's army into Ladysmith, one of the outstanding events of the Boer War (1899–1902). Britain's fortunes in this war first helped the Conservatives—who won the Khaki election 1900—but later proved a liability as people began to ask why Great Britain, with aid from India and some of the White Dominions, had taken so long to defeat an irregular army of Boer farmers

But Rhodes and his imperial supporters were not only interested in the fate of the unemployed. They also saw imperial development as a profitable investment for their own capital. As J. A. Hobson reported in 1902:

A nation may either . . . put brains into agriculture, develop a finely varied system of public education, general and technical, apply . . . science to its . . . manufacturing industries, and so support in progressive comfort and character a considerable population upon a strictly limited area; or it may, like Great Britain, neglect its agriculture, allowing its lands to go out of cultivation and its population to grow up in towns, fall behind other nations in its methods of education and in the capacity of adapting to its uses the latest scientific knowledge, in order that it may squander its . . . resources in forcing investment in distant corners of the earth, adding millions of square miles and of un-assimilable population to the area of the Empire.

Arrogance

Rhodes had declared that 'we are the best race' when explaining his support for imperial expansion. This claim is also reflected in the popular 'Land of Hope and Glory' with its claim that 'God hath made thee mighty' and its hope that 'Wider still and wider shall thy bounds be set'. The popular poet of the Empire was Rudyard Kipling, who wrote the following for the Queen's Jubilee, 1897:

God of our fathers, known of old,
Lord of our far-flung battle-line,
Beneath whose awful Hand we hold
Dominion over palm and pine—
Lord God of Hosts, be with us yet,
Lest we forget—lest we forget!

For heathen heart that puts her trust
In reeking tube and iron shard,
All valiant dust that builds on dust,
And guarding, calls not Thee to guard,
For frantic boast and foolish word—
Thy mercy on Thy People, Lord!

The tragedy was that most people did not heed the last line of the first verse, nor the last two lines of the final verse.

6 New Liberals and Old Tories

Chamberlain the Imperialist

Joseph Chamberlain, once radical Mayor of Birmingham and formerly 'Republican Joe', split the Liberal Party in 1886 and led his Liberal Unionists into the ranks of the Conservative Party which became known as the Conservative and Unionist Party. Chamberlain had once led the campaign against Disraeli's imperialism, claiming that the policy of expansion was being run on behalf of shareholders and not the British people. In 1895 he became Colonial Secretary in Salisbury's government and the Conservative Party revealed its capacity to absorb rebels.

Even before taking office he showed that he, too, had caught the bug of imperialism—for business reasons. In 1894 he said: 'in order that we may have more employment to give we must create more demand . . . new markets shall be created and . . . old markets shall be effectually developed'.

PUNCH, OR THE LONDON CHARIVARI.—DECEMBER 13, 1899.

34 Lord Salisbury had had his troubles with Lord Randolph Churchill in the 1880s. In the 1890s he had more trouble from Joseph Chamberlain, the former Liberal who had joined the Tory Party after splitting the Liberals over Gladstone's Irish policy

THE MEDDLESOME BOY.

JOE (*to himself*). "WONDER HOW IT'S GETTING ON!"
LORD S-L-SB-RY (*Head Gardener*). "I DO WISH HE'D LET THINGS ALONE!"

FOLLOW ME, LEADER.

THE HIND LEGS (*log*). "MY DEAR ARTHUR, OF COURSE YOU'RE THE ONLY CONCEIVABLE *HEAD*; BUT WE'RE GOING *MY* WAY!"

35 Joseph Chamberlain, the former radical Liberal became the outstanding Conservative imperialist in the late 1890s. However this ambitious politician could not be contained inside the bounds of the Party, which he split over the issue of Tariff Reform in 1903. His break with Glad-stone had created an opportunity for the Conservatives to get back into office in 1886; his break with Balfour helped the Liberals to win the 1906 election

Imperialism and tariffs

Germany, the USA and other countries protected their home markets from foreign (including British) competition by putting taxes on imports. Tariffs increase the price of the imported articles and so help to make home produced articles a better buy. But Britain was a Free Trade country which allowed foreign goods to be imported freely. In the 1880s a Fair Trade League was set up which asked that Britain should give up her policy of Free Trade, set up a system of tariffs and bargain with foreign countries, promising to lower our tariffs against their goods if they lowered their tariffs against British goods. This League had no success; the country had become great because of Free Trade; even Disraeli had recognised that 'protection is dead and damned'.

Chamberlain, as Colonial Secretary, became convinced that Britain would have to give up the Free Trade policy. His plan was to impose duties on foreign goods while at the same time building up trade with the Empire by a system of pre-ferential tariffs. Britain would ask Australia and the other territories in the Empire to put a lower tariff on British goods than on German goods; in return she would impose a lower tariff on their exports than on similar exports from, say, Denmark. Never one to do anything by halves, Chamberlain resigned from the Cabinet in 1903 to give himself the freedom to organise a tariff reform campaign. Speaking in Glasgow in October 1903, he declared:

49

If you will compare your trade in 1872, thirty years ago, with the trade of 1902—the export trade—you will find that there has been a moderate increase of £22,000,000. That is, something like seven and a half per cent. Meanwhile, the population has increased thirty per cent. . . . In the same time the increase in the United States of America was £110,000,000 and the increase in Germany was £56,000,000. In the United Kingdom our export trade has been practically stagnant for thirty years. . . .

Our imperial trade is absolutely essential to our prosperity at the present time. If that trade . . . does not increase in proportion to our population and to the loss of trade with foreign countries, then we sink at once into a fifth-rate nation. . . .

I have told you what you are to gain by preference . . . the increase of your customers . . . work for the enormous number of those who are now unemployed. . . . What will it cost? What do the colonies ask? They ask a preference on their particular products . . . you must put a tax on food.

This threat to Free Trade succeeded in reuniting a Liberal Party which had split in the late 1890s after Gladstone had retired. One wing of the Party had wanted to support a policy of imperialism; a more radical wing led by Lloyd George was opposed to this. Both wings were able to agree to oppose Chamberlain's policy of tariff reform. Even his own Conservative Party was unable to accept his ideas and as a divided Party they lost the 1906 election.

It is one of the ironies of the twentieth century that Neville Chamberlain, the son of the tariff reform campaigner, was the Chancellor of the Exchequer who, in 1932, ended Britain's Free Trade system. It had taken the Tory Party almost thirty years to get Disraeli's ideas across to the country; it took almost as long for Chamberlain's ideas to become acceptable.

The House of Lords—rebels?

The Liberals won a massive majority in the 1906 election and the Conservatives under Balfour were unable to prevent the passage through the Commons of a number of radical measures—on education, Church disestablishment, licensing laws and so on. But the Conservative minority in the Commons knew that there was a Conservative majority in the Lords which would see to it that these measures never got passed into law. As Balfour said in 1907: 'the real discussion of this question is not now in this House; . . . everybody is perfectly reconciled to the fact that . . . the Lords are going to deal with the Bill'.

This was not the first time on which the Lords had used their power to thwart Liberal hopes. They had threatened to do so in the 1860s when Gladstone reduced the stamp duty on newspapers—the Lords wanted to keep this duty which made newspapers expensive. Gladstone had to threaten the Lords before they allowed the Bill to go through. But in 1893 they had voted down his Second Home Rule for Ireland Bill. He had then coined the saying that 'the Lords must amend or be amended'. But no one took much notice because the Conservatives got back into power in 1895 and there was no clash between the Lords and the Commons. Now, however, with a Liberal majority the Lords were using their power.

The question being posed by the Lords' actions was: Is Britain a democracy governed by a Parliament elected by the people? Or is it an oligarchy governed by a hereditary House of Lords which can obstruct the work of the people's House?

The Budget, 1909

In 1908 Parliament approved the first Old Age Pensions Act; this awarded 25p per week to everyone over the age of 70 provided that they had little or no income from other sources. This was the first of the steps taken by the Liberals to lay the foundations of the modern Welfare State. They were already planning the opening of Labour Exchanges, the introduction of the Health Service and of an Unemployment Insurance Scheme. All this, plus the rebuilding of the British fleet, was to cost a good deal. In 1909 Lloyd George was Chancellor of the Exchequer. His first Budget was, he said, 'a war against poverty' to be paid for by increased taxation. Income tax was raised, a new super-tax was imposed, taxes on spirits were increased and a new land tax was promised. All these were opposed by the aristocratic House of Lords.

Lloyd George warned the country of what the Lords might do to the Budget. Speaking in Newcastle in October, 1909, he said:

> Should 500 men . . . override the judgment . . . of millions of people who are engaged in the industry which makes the wealth of the country? . . . Who made 10,000 people owners, and the rest of us trespassers in the land of our birth? Who is responsible for the scheme . . . whereby one man is engaged through life in grinding labour . . . and when, at the end of his days, he claims . . . a poor pension of eight pence a day . . . can only get it through a revolution; and another man, who does not (toil), receives every hour of the day, every hour of the night, whilst he slumbers, more than his neighbours . . . in a whole year of toil?

The Conservatives had not only inherited the Liberal philosophy of Free Trade; they had also taken over the Liberal belief in lower taxation as an end in itself.

The Lords put down

The Budget was rejected in the Lords and this led to a general election in January 1910. The Liberals won 274 seats to the Conservatives' 273. The balance of power in the Commons was held by the Irish with 82 seats and the Labour Party with 40 seats. The Irish promised to support the Liberals—and get the Budget through the Commons—if they were promised another Home Rule Bill and a Bill which would limit the power of the Lords—who had thrown out Gladstone's Home Rule Bill.

A second election in December 1910 left party representation much as it had been. This election was called for because after the death of King Edward VII, his successor, George V, was unwilling to throw his weight behind the Liberals

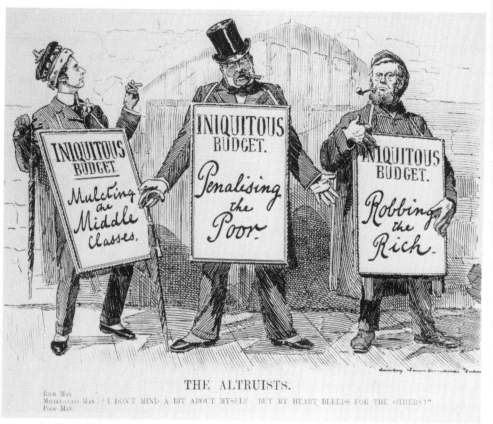

THE ALTRUISTS.

RICH MAN
MIDDLE-CLASS MAN : "I DON'T MIND A BIT ABOUT MYSELF; BUT MY HEART BLEEDS FOR THE OTHERS!"
POOR MAN

36 A *Punch* cartoon of May 1909, issued while the Commons were debating Lloyd George's Budget. This promised to increase taxation as a means of getting the money required to lay the foundations of the Welfare State

until the people had had another chance to vote on the issue of 'the Peers or the people'. In 1911 the King agreed to help the Liberals get their Bill through the Lords by promising to create as many as five hundred new Liberal Peers.

The passage of this Parliament Act in 1911 was the logical outcome of the various parliamentary reforms of the nineteenth century. As Disraeli had foreseen, the House of Commons now dominated the political scene.

The Lords and Ireland

In 1912 the Irish got their promised Home Rule Bill which, because of the passage of the Parliament Act, would become law in 1914. The Conservatives had always opposed Irish home rule. Randolph Churchill, in 1886, had coined the slogan 'Ulster will fight and Ulster will be right'. In 1912 the Conservative leader was Bonar Law, a Canadian Presbyterian of Scots origin. His background made him very sympathetic to the Ulster Protestants and, at a massive rally at the Blenheim home of the Duke of Marlborough, he announced: 'they would be justified in resisting by all means in their power, including force. I can imagine no length of resistance to which Ulster will go in which I shall not be ready to support them'.

At about the same time the Ulster Covenant was being signed by the Protestants

52

37 Bonar Law, who became leader of the Conservative Party after Balfour, was forced to resign in 1911. He was born in Canada in 1858, the son of a Presbyterian minister who had emigrated from Ulster. He had been brought up in Glasgow where he had made a considerable fortune as an iron merchant. He was the first industrialist to get to the top in the Conservative Party

38 Sir Edward Carson (centre, walking) and a fellow MP, F. E. Smith (later Lord Birkenhead) being cheered at their arrival at an Anti-Home Rule meeting, September 1912.

of Northern Ireland who pledged themselves to stand together in defending their citizenship of the United Kingdom and who declared that they would use any means to defeat the passage of the Home Rule Bill and its imposition upon them.

The leader of the rebel movement was Sir Edward Carson, a lawyer, and soon to be Attorney General in a Coalition government. He persuaded British Army Officers to resign rather than take up the fight against their Ulster 'kith and kin'. Writing to his leader, Bonar Law, in March 1914, he said: 'a very large number of officers all over Ireland resigned. . . . I understand that a large body . . . have consented to remain on, on condition that they are not expected to act in Ulster . . . I hear now that a large number of non-commissioned officers and men are saying that nothing will induce them to take sides against Ulster'.

The Curragh mutiny

It seems a far cry from the days when all anti-government activities were considered revolutionary (Chapter 2). In 1914 the Lords, the Conservative Opposition, the Army and the Irish Protestants were united in an anti-Liberal movement which seemed bound to lead to a bloody civil war in Ireland.

War, 1914

The war that came was not between Ulster Protestants and a Liberal government. In August 1914 Germany, already at war with France, attacked Belgium, whom Britain had pledged to defend. Britain declared war on Germany and the country which had seemed so divided suddenly found itself united again in the face of a common enemy. Asquith invited Bonar Law and leading Conservatives to join him in a Coalition government where they sat with their peace time enemy, Lloyd George. Even more significantly, when Asquith proved incapable of leading the country, the Conservatives agreed to serve under Lloyd George.

The war and the Conservatives

The Liberal Party was badly split as a result of the war; some members, such as Wedgwood and Morley, resigned from the government rather than give up their pacifism; many followed Asquith in his opposition to Lloyd George who was regarded by them as a traitor when he took over in 1916; a third group followed Lloyd George. Equally, the Labour Party was split, with some following MacDonald in total opposition to the war, while a less-radical group followed Henderson and Clynes, who served in Lloyd George's government. Only the Conservatives emerged unscathed from the war. Here, as under Disraeli, they were the patriotic party. They had their reward in the election of 1918 when Lloyd George led a Coalition government to a sweeping victory over the Asquithian Liberals and the Labour Party:

Conservative and Unionist	338 seats
Lloyd George's Liberals	116 seats
Labour	57 seats
Asquithian Liberals	26 seats

The Conservative Party had become the party of the middle class; the Liberal Party had been split and squeezed.

39 Crowds in London cheering the declaration of war, 1914. By 1918 the crowds were less confident, more sombre and less 'patriotic', which helps to explain the general support for Chamberlain's appeasement policy

Party conflict again

By 1922 many Conservative backbenchers wanted to break with Lloyd George. But Lloyd George had persuaded the leading Conservatives to stay in the Coalition for the next general election. The Conservative Party workers represented in the National Union of Conservative Associations were strongly against this attempt to create a centre party. They were due to have their annual meeting on 15

40 Lloyd George (centre) with French Prime Minister Briand and Marshall Foch in 1921, when Lloyd George was still Prime Minister of a predominantly Conservative government. The photograph was taken at Chequers, the Prime Minister's country residence which was given to the nation by Sir Arthur Lee in time for Lloyd George to enjoy the house before his fall in 1922

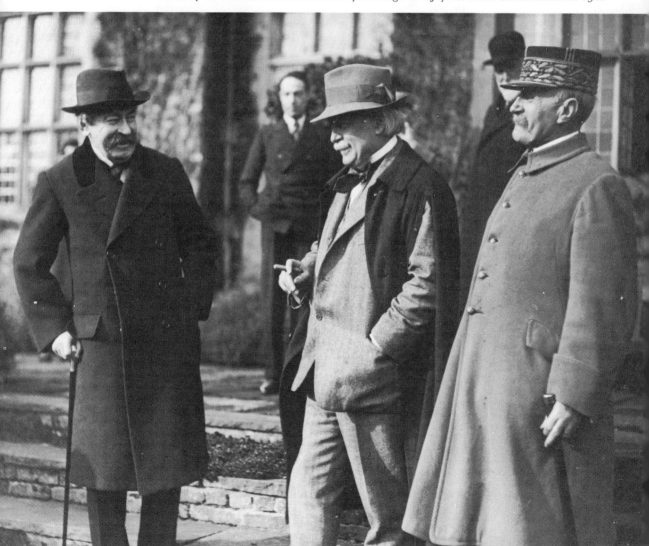

41 Stanley Baldwin outside 10 Downing Street. He was Prime Minister in 1923, 1925–29 and 1935–37. The country and the Party owed a great deal to the moderation of this man

November, when a demand would be made for the Party to leave the Coalition. Conservatives in the Coalition decided to forestall this by calling a meeting of all Conservative MPs and Peers at the Carlton Club on 19 October. Here, it was hoped, a vote of confidence in the Coalition government would be carried. If this were done the National Union would realise that its duty was to support the leadership (page 42).

The only Conservative Minister to oppose the continuation of the Coalition was Stanley Baldwin. Referring to a description of the Prime Minister as a 'dynamic force', Baldwin told the Carlton Club: 'A dynamic force is a very terrible thing; it may crush you, but it is not necessarily right. It is owing to that dynamic force . . . that the Liberal Party to which he formerly belonged, has been smashed to pieces; and it is my firm conviction that in time, the same thing will happen to our Party'.

The vote showed that the majority wanted to end the Coalition; Chamberlain and other leaders refused to accept this decision. When the 1922 election resulted in a Conservative victory, Bonar Law had to call on the 'second eleven' to form a government in which no leading Conservatives would serve.

Tory businessmen

When Bonar Law was forced to retire owing to ill-health after a short period in office, Baldwin became Prime Minister (1923) and called another election. Faced with growing unemployment, Baldwin had become a convert to tariff reform. He said: 'To me, at least, this unemployment problem is the most critical problem of our country. . . . And I have come to the conclusion myself that the only way of fighting this subject is by protecting the home market'.

Although the Conservatives still won the largest number of seats they were unable to command a majority in the Commons; Baldwin, therefore, advised King George V to ask MacDonald to form a Labour government. In 1924 this first Labour government was defeated and Baldwin was back again as Prime Minister. This time he amazed everyone by appointing Winston Churchill as Chancellor of the Exchequer. As one of the Coalition Conservatives wrote: 'The one dominant motive all through with him was fear of Lloyd George and his influence. . . . It was fear of LG's influence, combined with Winston's, over Austen [Chamberlain] and FE [Smith] that led to the amazing offer of the Exchequer to Winston. Later on, in 1931, it was largely to keep out Winston and Lloyd George that he consented to the no less disastrous Coalition with Ramsay MacDonald'.

It was Churchill, supported by the businessmen, who in 1925 decided to revalue the pound sterling as a means of helping the City of London to regain its place as the world's leading money market. But reflation meant an increase in the price of British exports as the following example shows:

Assume that the price of a British car is £200.

42 The anti-tariff election, 1923. The Liberal candidate here at Devonport was Leslie Hore-Belisha. He became a member of the Coalition government under Baldwin and Chamberlain in the 1930s. He is best remembered for the Belisha beacons which mark pedestrain crossings

If the exchange rate is $4.02 to £1, price in USA = $804
$4.80 to £1, price in USA = $960

At the higher price fewer British goods were bought and there was more un-employment. Manufacturers, anxious to maintain, if not increase, the volume of their exports tried to get British prices back to the same or even to a lower level than that which they had reached before revaluation. The only way in which this could be done was by asking workmen to accept huge wage cuts—and this was the main cause of the General Strike in 1926.

The Commons were dominated by men who had profited from the war; Baldwin may have thought that these businessmen would produce a businesslike solution to the country's economic problems. Instead, they tried to turn the clock back; they looked back to the 'golden days' of the nineteenth century and tried to recreate the conditions which had helped Britain to become the world's leading investor. The Conservative yearning for tradition may sometimes be a good thing, but the hard-faced men were yearning for the wrong things.

Tariff reform

The country had not given Baldwin the majority he hoped for in the 1923 tariff reform election, and so he refused to raise the matter in the 1924 and 1929 elections. The Labour government of 1923–24 and 1929–31 was equally opposed to giving up Free Trade, although as Iain Macleod said:

[In 1931] a strong movement of opinion, now no longer confined to the Conservative Party, manifested itself in favour of a tariff. Not only the Federation of British Industries but also the economic committee of the Trades Union Congress, not only Oswald Mosley . . . but also Maynard Keynes and John Simon . . . were saying the same thing in different ways. But to all these voices the government and its obstinate Chancellor, Philip Snowden, shut their ears. 'The reflection which came to me', said Neville Chamberlain in the Budget debate on 28 April, 'was that here is the last Chancellor of the Exchequer who will ever again introduce a Free Trade Budget in this House'. His words were . . . certainly prophetic.

Chamberlain became Chancellor in the National government which was formed when the Labour Party split over the financial crisis of 1931 (see below). On 4 February 1932, which he described as 'the greatest day of my life', he addressed the Commons. Iain Macleod records:

He took the notes from the red dispatch box which had been his father's as Colonial Secretary. A general tariff, he claimed, would . . . decrease unemployment by transferring 'to our own factories work which is now done elsewhere'. He therefore moved that there should be charged on all goods imported save those specifically exempted, a duty of 10 per cent of their value. . . . None of the new duties would apply to goods from the Dominions. Then, he came to the peroration:

'There can have been few occasions when to the son has been vouchsafed the privilege of setting the seal on the work which the father began. . . . His work was not in vain . . . I believe he would have found consolation for the bitterness of his disappointment if he could have foreseen that these proposals would be laid before the House of Commons in the presence of one and by the lips of the other of his sons'.

Austen came down and silently shook hands with his brother while the House cheered and cheered again. (*From 'Neville Chamberlain' by Iain Macleod, published by Muller.*)

The Conservatives and Labour

One of the remarkable features of post-war Britain was the rise of the Labour Party to a prominent position; Labour replaced the Liberals as the alternative to the Conservatives; in 1923 MacDonald formed his first government and in

43 The lighter side of the General Strike 1926. A team of policemen played a team of strikers at Plymouth Argyle's ground; the strikers won 2–1, their only success in this 'English Revolution'

1929 his second. Many people, including Lloyd George, were anxious to keep Labour out of power—this was one of his reasons for wanting to form a centre party. But Baldwin realised that if about half the electorate supported a party which was then refused a chance to hold office, there might very well be a revolution. He also realised that the Labour Party was not a 'wild', 'red', or 'Bolshevik-dominated' party, as many of his fellow Conservatives believed. Indeed, he had a special affection for many of the older working-class MPs. As Labour Prime Minister, Attlee recalled: 'He always seemed more at home with our people, particularly the older trade union people, than with his own lot'.

Conservatives and red revolution

Baldwin's government announced that it would no longer give a subsidy to the mine owners. The owners decided to pass the burden on to the miners themselves by demanding a longer working day for less money. They replied with 'not a penny off the pay, not a minute on the day' and in May 1926 the Trade Union Congress announced that they would support the miners' case. A General Strike was called and the clash between the miners and the owners expanded into a clash between the TUC and the government. One government spokesman called it 'a direct challenge to ordered government and a direct hold-up of the nation to ransom'. Baldwin himself said: 'Constitutional government is being attacked . . . The

General Strike is a challenge to Parliament and is the road to ruin'. A union spokesman, on the other hand, argued that the General Council did not challenge the Constitution but that its sole aim was to secure a decent standard of life for the miners.

Some union leaders may have thought that they were engaged in a struggle to create a workers' republic. Few shared their opinion and the Strike fizzled out after only nine days. The TUC ordered a return to work and apart from the miners, most people went back. This absence of revolutionary activity marks Britain off from the rest of Europe in the 1920s and 1930s. Elsewhere there were either Communist or Fascist dictatorships, risings and movements. Britain escaped largely because of Baldwin's success in persuading working people that the Conservative Party was not anti-worker. He believed that both extremes of political thought could be avoided if his own Party accepted liberalised Toryism as a middle position.

Coalition again

In 1929 the Labour Party won 288 seats; for the first time it was the largest Party in the Commons although it did not have a majority since the Conservatives had 260 seats and the various wings of the Liberal Party had 59. The British bankers, eager to get back their place as the world's leading investing centre, had been borrowing money from various European and American banks in order to lend it out again to other people. In 1931 the world's banking system received a shock as the leading Austrian bank was forced to close, owing millions to people who had trusted this system. Austrian, French, American and German banks now began to fear that British banks might suffer the same experience; so they demanded the immediate repayment of their loans to Britain. To try to allay these fears the

44 Ramsay MacDonald leading his Coalition Cabinet down the steps into the garden of 10 Downing Street. He is followed by J. H. Thomas (Labour), Lord Reading (Liberal), Stanley Baldwin and Snowden, formerly Labour's Chancellor of the Exchequer. At the top of the steps from left to right are Sir Philip Cunliffe-Lister, Neville Chamberlain (a future Prime Minister and son of Joseph) and, wearing a hat, Sir Herbert Samuel a former Liberal

45 Edward, Prince of Wales, talking to unemployed miners during his visit to Abertillery, South Wales, 1936. The decline in Britain's old industries (coal, cotton, steel, ship-building) helped to create the depressed areas of Wales, Scotland and Northern England. The Prince of Wales is supposed to have said 'Something must be done'—but very little was

British government tried to balance the 1931 Budget—always a sign of financial strength—by cutting government spending on unemployment benefit.

The Labour Cabinet was split over the proposals. MacDonald went to Buckingham Palace to resign. When he returned to 10 Downing Street, to speak to the assembled Cabinet Ministers who had been summoned there, he shocked them by telling them that the King had invited him to form a National government and that he had accepted. Few Labour MPs followed MacDonald, who found himself at the head of a National (or Coalition) government, dominated by Conservatives. This domination was confirmed when first Baldwin (1935) and later, Neville Chamberlain, became Prime Minister. The resignation of the Labour government and the formation of the National government did nothing to halt the continued rise in the level of unemployment. From mid-1931 until July 1933 the monthly unemployment figures never fell below 3 million. Britain had to endure the 'great depression' while governments seemed powerless to do anything to bring work to the people.

This depression was a major reason for the crushing defeat suffered by the Conservatives in the 1945 election. It is often forgotten that the inter-war years, dominated as they were by Conservative governments, were years during which the Welfare State developed. Neville Chamberlain was particularly active. His biographer recalls that the National Health Insurance Act of 1928 brought 'added help to some sixteen and a half million men and women workers. In four years 440 more Infant Welfare Centres were opened and 300 more antenatal clinics, while the number of practising midwives increased by 860. The infant mortality rate, 132 per 1,000 live births in 1906, 75 in 1924, was 65 in 1928. . . . There was legislation on clean food, clean water and clean air as well as the important Public Health Act of 1925. The "policy of sewage" inspired by Disraeli was in good hands'.

Foreign affairs

The party of imperialism and patriotism went through a series of bad patches in the 1920s and 1930s. The various commissions and reports on India indicated that in the future India would become a self–governing country, as were Australia and other former 'white colonies'. The British retreat from imperial power had begun. Equally, there was a retreat from activity in foreign affairs. The opinions of the ruling classes were dominated by a fear of revolution, inspired by the rise

46 A Welfare Officer visiting a house in Hoxton, London. Many people think that the Welfare State was started by the Liberals and finished off by Labour between 1945 and 1951. In fact the Welfare State was developed during the inter-war period and Neville Chamberlain in particular has a claim to be considered one of its architects

47 Neville Chamberlain (left) with the German dictator, Adolf Hitler at Berchtesgaden, September 1938. This was the first of three visits by Chamberlain to Germany; the last of them, when he went to Munich, ended with the dismemberment of Czechoslovakia. Chamberlain reflected the wish of the British people for peace rather than war against the German dictator. When he returned from Munich he reminded the crowd of Disraeli's success at the 1878 Congress of Berlin. 'This is the second time that there has come back from Germany to Downing Street peace with honour' and the crowd roared their approval of Bolshevik Russia, as well as by the memories of the slaughter of 1914–18. Public opinion in general was dominated by similar bitter war-time memories which produced the resolution that such a war should never happen again. This explains the refusal to take any active steps to prevent Hitler breaking the clauses of the Treaty of Versailles, which he did when he marched into the Rhineland, invaded Austria and conquered Czechoslovakia. When Chamberlain flew to Germany to submit to Hitler's demands most British people wished him well. As Iain Macleod wrote:

> Chamberlain returned from Germany to a hero's welcome . . . the streets, as the Prime Minister described to his sisters, 'were lined from one end to the other with people of every class, shouting themselves hoarse, leaping on the running board, banging on the windows, and thrusting their hands into the car to be shaken'. . . . Later, under his window in Downing Street, densely packed crowds sang: 'For he's a jolly good fellow'.
> (*From 'Neville Chamberlain' by Iain Macleod, published by Muller.*)

Few people shared the opinions of Churchill who, in the Commons, said: 'I will begin by saying the most unpopular and unwelcome thing. I will begin by saying what everybody would like to ignore or forget but which must nevertheless be stated, namely that we have sustained a total and unmitigated defeat'.

It is significant that Neville Chamberlain was not finally overthrown until May 1940, when Germany had already conquered Norway and Denmark. During a debate on these disasters many Conservatives were eager to speak out against the Prime Minister. However, it was left to a Labour MP to get up and move a motion of censure on the Prime Minister. As he rose to speak, Leo Amery, a Conservative MP, shouted 'Speak for the people of England'—a far cry from the days when it was the Tories who did so and the radicals who opposed the patriotic Party.

8   Churchill and a Modern Party, 1949-1955

The surprising election result, 1945

In May 1940 Winston Churchill became Prime Minister of a Coalition government
and leader of the Conservative Party. In May 1945 the Germans surrendered
and the war in Europe was over. Churchill asked the Labour Ministers in his
Coalition to stay on until Japan was defeated; they refused and asked that a
general election be fought as soon as possible. The date fixed was 5 July 1945,
although the results were not announced until 25 July to allow for the counting
of votes from service people scattered across the world.

Churchill and the Conservatives hoped to repeat in 1945 the victory which
Lloyd George, the other war-winner, had achieved in 1918. Wherever he went,
Churchill met tremendous and enthusiastic crowds. But when the votes were counted the Labour Party had won a sweeping victory with 393 to 213 for the Conservatives, and Attlee formed the first Labour government with a Commons majority.

One important reason for this defeat was people's memories of the 1920s and
1930s when the country had been ruled by Conservative or Conservative-
dominated governments. Rightly or wrongly people blamed them for the unemployment and misery. Linked with this was the second important reason:
people's expectations were much greater in 1945 than they had been in the past.

48   Winston Churchill, British Prime Minister, arriving back in London after his sea conference
with American President Roosevelt in August 1941

Between 1940 and 1945 the government had set up a system whereby expectant mothers could get cheap milk, free vitamins and medical attention; young children were given free orange juice and other foods at welfare clinics; a system of family allowances was introduced in 1945 to help raise the living standards of larger families. During the war there was no unemployment: on the contrary there were high wages and plenty of work for women as well as men. There was also the Beveridge Report, which had come out in 1942 from a Commission, set up by the Churchill government, to examine the social services. Beveridge showed that there were five 'Great Evils' which could affect people's lives—Want (or poverty), Disease, Ignorance, Idleness (or unemployment) and Squalor (or bad housing). He showed how each of these 'Giants' could be overcome by government action: Want, for example, would be slain by a policy of full employment and by a system of National Insurance; Disease could be slain by a National Health Service.

During the war the government had mobilised the nation's resources for the purpose of defeating the military enemy. Beveridge asked that a similar mobilisation be used to overcome social evils. In 1945 people were not only looking back in anger at the 1930s; they were also looking expectantly to a period when there would be no unemployment, more council houses, a free Health Service. In 1945, rightly or wrongly, the majority of people believed that they were more likely to get these from a Labour government.

49 Unemployed in Wigan in the 1930s. This was the fate of millions of British workmen in the 1920s and 1930s. During this time the country was ruled by Conservative or Conservative-dominated governments and memories of this long period of depression were largely responsible for the Conservative defeat in the 1945 election

50 Winston Churchill speaking at the Conservative Party Conference, October 1947. Behind sits Lord Woolton who was called in by Churchill to reorganise the Party so that it would be fit to fight and win the next election

Defeat and reorganisation

When the House of Commons assembled, a new Labour MP, Hartley Shawcross, yelled across the floor 'We are the masters now'. It is one of the ironies of the post-war period that this fervent Labourite became a leading spokesman for the Conservatives in the 1970s—proving yet again the capacity of the Conservatives to absorb their enemies. But in 1945 the Conservatives needed to put their Party in order, so that they could fight the confident Labour Party.

Churchill asked Lord Woolton, a wartime colleague, to take charge of one aspect of this reorganisation. Woolton was the chairman of Lewis's, the Manchester store —one of the successful middle–class businessmen who would probably have been a Liberal in the nineteenth century; but such men had become Conservatives as they grew richer. Woolton appealed to British businessmen, and raised one million pounds as a fighting fund; he examined the Party constituency organisation and appointed a number of full-time, paid agents in certain constituencies. Their job was to work up enthusiasm, to encourage people to join the Party as active workers so that the electoral machine would be stronger in 1950 when the next election took place. Woolton also helped to found the Young Conservatives; in the 1930s most young people had been left-wing; this was another reason for Labour's victory in the 1945 election—they had most of the first-time voters. By founding the YCs, Woolton hoped to attract many first voters into the Conservative machine. He also hoped that they would be active workers in the election campaigns.

The machine had to have ammunition. R. A. Butler, a former Minister of Education, took charge of the Conservative Central Office and, with assistance of bright young men such as Reginald Maudling and Enoch Powell, drew up a series of documents outlining Conservative policy. In this way the Conservatives produced leaflets and pamphlets showing the electorate how they would run the country.

The Conservatives and social change

Speaking to the Young Conservatives Conference in 1949, Robert Boothby, MP, said that the country had gone through 'the greatest social revolution in its history' since the Labour Party had taken office. R. A. Butler said: 'I think we should take pride that the British race has been able, shortly after the terrible period (1939–45) through which we have passed together, to show the world that we are able to produce a Social Insurance Scheme of this character'. In fact, the Coalition government—including the Labour Ministers Attlee and Morrison—had not been enthusiastic when the Beveridge Report had first appeared. The Conservatives, in Opposition after 1945, had opposed the passage of the various Bills required to bring the Health Service and other schemes into operation. But one of the outstanding features of Conservatism, as we have seen, is its capacity to amend its attitudes and policies to fit the needs of the moment.

Even in 1953 there were a large number of people who resented the changes that had resulted in 'the greatest social revolution'. Sir Philip Gibbs, a leading

51 Sir Edward (now Lord) Boyle visiting a school for handicapped children in 1953. Boyle was one of the many 'liberal' Conservatives who were given a place in Conservative governments in the 1950s

journalist and author, wrote: 'I for one rejoice in the new prosperity of the great mass of people in this country. . . . An illusion is there, alas. . . . But one thing is fairly certain: the prospect of a continuance of high taxation and low-level living'.

He reflected the opinion of many middle-class people who had enjoyed a high standard of living in the 1930s owing to low wages and falling prices, but who now saw their standard of living affected by higher wages and taxation, and who also saw many manual workers enjoying a continually higher standard of living. John Gunther was an American writer who reported on his visit to Britain in the mid-1950s:

> Everybody has money. . . . Wages have gone up and never before has the working class had such spending power. . . . Another point is the enormous increase of hire purchase. This puts merchandise in the reach of almost everybody and it is another reason why classes are being levelled out. . . . Financial drain caused by severe . . . or prolonged illness is now all but eliminated, which is not only a good thing of itself but releases immense funds for other use. (*From 'Inside Europe Today' by John Gunther, published by Hamish Hamilton.*)

Freedom

One of the slogans used by the reorganised Conservatives was 'Set the people free' —from taxation, restrictions, rationing and controls. In 1951 the Conservatives were back in power again, winning 321 seats to Labour's 295, while the Liberals had only 6 seats. This emphasis on freedom is a relic of the link-up between Toryism and Liberalism in the nineteenth century (page 45). It is at odds with Disraeli's idea of the duty of a government to interfere to ensure the good life for the people. An American once told Beveridge that if there had been social security in the days of Elizabeth I there would have been no Raleigh, Drake or Hawkins. Beveridge's reply was 'Adventure came not from the half-starved, but from those who were well-enough fed to feel ambition'. Freedom from want was the privilege of a minority in sixteenth-century England; Beveridge and the socialists wanted this freedom extended to everyone. The Conservatives suggested in their election propaganda that this freedom was being bought at the price of high taxation and great interference.

However, Conservatism in practice turned out to be different from that preached in the pamphlets on freedom. Most voters expected to maintain their high standard of living—so there was little a government could do about taxation which supported the Health Service and so on. Indeed, so similar were these Conservative policies (with Butler as Chancellor) to those of their Labour predecessors (when Gaitskell was Chancellor), that a new word was coined. *Butskellism* was journalists' shorthand for the Conservative-socialist policies followed by Churchill and his Conservative government. As one radio comic said:

'Have you seen Jimmy's new suit? It's a conservative cut.'

'What's a conservative cut?'
'It's the same as a socialist cut, only they are more polite about it.'

Empire

This was an attempt to find a middle ground where Conservatism has much in common with Labour. However, between the two main parties there was apparently a great difference in their attitudes towards the Empire and Commonwealth. Between 1945 and 1950 the Labour government had given independence to India, Pakistan, Ceylon and Burma. In 1948 the British government had given up its mandate in Palestine in the face of hostility from both Jew and Arab. In 1950–51 the Labour government allowed the Persian government to nationalise the oilfields of the Anglo-Iranian Oil Company and drive the British out of Persia (Iran). All these 'retreats' were opposed by the Conservatives.

In 1951 Churchill took office, saying: 'I have not become the King's First Minister to preside over the liquidation of the British Empire'. But it was his government which made an agreement with Egypt by which Britain withdrew her forces from the Suez Canal Area (1954). It was also a Conservative government, with Anthony Eden as Prime Minister, which went to war with Egypt in 1956 after the nationalisation of the Suez Canal—'the lifeline of Empire'—which had been built by the French but which was now owned by an Anglo-French Company.

When the British invaded Egypt on 30 October 1956 the *Daily Telegraph* said: 'How good it is to hear the British Lion's roar'. The *Sunday Express* called it: 'The proudest week we have known for years'. But within a week the British government had to call a halt to its invasion in the face of opposition from the United Nations Organisation, the USA and Russia. It was no longer possible for a Conservative government to act as Disraeli had done in the 1870s. The Suez disaster marks the end—or at least the beginning of the end—of Britain's claim to be a first-class world power. Even Conservatives had to accept this, and within a short space of time Ghana, Tanganyika, Zambia, Kenya and other African colonies had been given their freedom by Conservative governments. In this, as in social welfare, there was not a great deal of difference between Labour and Conservative governments.

The beginnings of modern Britain

If the mid-1950s marked the end of Britain's claims to be a world power, it also marked the beginnings of several new features which make modern Britain different from the old. It was in the mid–1950s that the modern problem of inflation became noticeable. As Lord Boothby pointed out in the House of Lords:

What are the main causes of our present trouble? The greatest has been excessive public expenditure ever since the war. I am oppressed by the expenditure on defence. . . . My second point . . . a system of progressive taxation on earned income. . . . Thirdly, the actions of employers and workers who are responsible

52 Prime Minister Anthony Eden (right) shakes hands with M. Pineau, French Prime Minister, at the entrance to 10 Downing Street on 18 September 1956, during the Suez crisis. In the centre is Selwyn Lloyd, British Foreign Minister. Aneurin Bevan, Labour's Shadow Foreign Minister, was attacking Lloyd's policy when Eden entered the House of Commons. Bevan broke off saying: 'It isn't fair to attack the monkey when the organ grinder is here'—indicating that Eden controlled the Foreign Office even after he became Prime Minister

for determining rates of wages and the prices which inevitably follow by bidding for higher wages.

(*From 'My Yesterday, Your Tomorrow' by Robert Boothby, published by Hutchinson.*)

53 A Vicky cartoon showing Eden giving in to a (Suez) temptation offered by an attractive France, only to find that the United Nations and an angelic President Eisenhower of the USA bring his brief happiness to a sad end. The cartoon appeared on 8 December 1956; Vicky was more accurate than he realised at the time because not only had the Franco-British adventure been brought to an end, but within a few weeks Eden had been forced to resign

Subsequent Conservative governments have done little to lessen the trouble of which Boothby spoke.

There were also the first signs of the advent of the so-called 'affluent society' in which more people could afford to buy more goods which manufacturers wanted them to buy. One method used by the manufacturers to attract the consumer was advertising. The introduction of commercial TV in 1954 and the growth in the number of coloured supplement magazines were features of this development. As Lord Samuel said in the House of Lords:

> Our modern twentieth-century civilisation is already far too much commercialised by the buying and selling of things that we use and consume. Advertisements have been intrusive everywhere for the last fifty years. . . . Now we have this new influence entering every home and affecting the environment of every family. Why should we, for the sake of picking up a million or two, degrade our broadcasting system with a continuous stream of commercial advertising? . . . Why should we sell the listening time of the nation to various wealthy commercial undertakings?

This is the voice of an Asquithian Liberal who seemed to resent the spread of 'buying and selling' to ordinary people. The Conservatives welcomed and promoted this growing prosperity.

Churchill's retirement

In 1953 Queen Elizabeth II came to the throne on the death of her father, George VI. In 1955 Winston Churchill decided to give up the leadership of the Conservative Party; in many ways he was a symbol of a bygone age—of Empire, aristocracy, British power. His retirement marks not only the end of one man's career; it is also the symbol of a change in Britain's fortunes. The new Conservatives were helping to create a new society in a semi-socialist Britain.

54 Harold Macmillan (centre) with Test Captains Ted Dexter (left) and Frank Worrell (right) of the West Indies, at the Prime Ministers official country home, Chequers, 1963

9 Macmillan and Liberal Conservatism

Conservatism in 1957

Anthony Eden resigned as Prime Minister after the failure of his Suez venture, and was succeeded by Harold Macmillan. As a Cabinet colleague recalled: 'When he became Prime Minister in January 1957 Harold Macmillan succeeded to a gloomy inheritance. At home the Conservative Party was split and shaken. Abroad, Great Britain had declined in stature and repute; the economic situation was rocky; and worst of all there had been a disastrous deterioration in Anglo-American relations'.

In addition to this 'gloomy inheritance' there were also problems about the future of the African colonies, as well as a problem about the way in which Conservatism was to develop in the future. Was it to go all out for the 'never had it so good' philosophy, promoting material benefits to the nation as a whole? If so, how was Conservatism to show itself different from socialism—which had much the same sort of aim? And how was this material improvement to be carried out? Was a Conservative government to continue to be an interfering, regulating, government—much as a socialist one would be? There were many Conservatives who thought that the Party should strike out on a fresh road for Britain—a non-socialist, non-interfering road which would also lead to the maintenance of the African Empire.

Macmillan and socialism

Macmillan had been MP for Stockton in the 1920s and 1930s. He had seen the depression at first hand, since his constituency was in one of the old industrial areas which suffered most from unemployment. In the 1930s he had been one of the small group of MPs who had called for greater government activity and spending as a means of creating more employment. Now, when he took over as Prime Minister, much of what he had asked for was already in operation. He recalled in his memoirs:

> It is very difficult for those whose memories do not go back to the twenties and thirties to have any conception of the virulence with which the role of the State in a modern economy was contested. . . . Any form of State intervention was believed to be necessarily incompetent, and the prelude to some form of dictatorship. Now we have a government which controls the central bank, and assumes responsibility for the general level of economic activity through the Bank rate and the Budget. . . . The era of strict *laissez faire* has passed into history,

55 R. A. Butler (centre), Deputy Prime Minister, and Harold Macmillan, Chancellor of the Exchequer, outside 10 Downing Street after a Cabinet meeting held during Eden's absence. One of these was to succeed Eden on his retirement; most people assumed that Butler would finally get to the top of the 'greasy pole' as Disraeli called it. However Macmillan proved more acceptable to the MPs and Conservative Lords who were asked to make the choice

together with the derelict towns, the boarded-up shops, and the barefooted children, and—above all—the long rows of men and women outside the Labour Exchanges.

One result of these and other changes had been a vast improvement in the general standard of living. Macmillan told the House of Commons in July 1957: 'Every Hon Member knows that for the mass of the people there has never been such a good time or such a high standard of living. I repeat what I said at Bedford, "They have never had it so good". I have been grateful to see the change. I believe that all of us in the House, certainly the older Members, feel grateful that there has been this great change'.

Macmillan and elections

Stanley Baldwin had taught the Conservative Party to look leftwards, to become more liberal-minded. One effect of this was that Britain did not suffer from the

Fascist–Communist clashes which affected Europe in the 1930s. Macmillan followed a similar policy of getting the Party to agree to semi–socialist policies in the 1950s. One sign of his success was the Party's victory in the 1959 general election. This was the first time in modern history that a Party had won three elections in succession (1951, 1955 and now 1959)—each time increasing its majority. It seemed that the Conservative Party, like the mass of the people, had 'never had it so good'. As David Butler wrote in the *British General Election, 1959* (published by Macmillan): 'The last ten years have eroded some of the traditional foundations of Labour strength. Full employment and the Welfare State have made the well-paid worker much less dependent on his trade union or on the Labour Party than before the war'.

Herbert Morrison, a Labour Party leader, recalls the 1959 election campaign:

Wherever I went I saw clever Tory posters portraying happy family scenes with the slogan: 'Life's better with the Conservatives—Don't let Labour ruin it'. . . . By the time that Parliament was dissolved this advertising, as well as

56 Macmillan during the 1959 election accompanied by Lady Dorothy Macmillan on a drive through Clapham, London

the Prime Minister's activities, had done a great deal of psychological pre-
paration. Very many people accepted that they had never had it so good. . . . The
1959 election was awaited with interest by observers of the British political scene
as the first where television would play a vital and predominant part.
(*From 'An Autobiography' by Herbert Morrison, published by Odhams.*)

Macmillan and economics

But increasing affluence brought its own problems, already evident before
Macmillan took over. As people had more money to spend so there were the twin
problems of an unfavourable balance of payments and inflation. Attempts to
solve these problems—the result of socialist-conservatism—led to Macmillan
setting up the National Economic Development Council ('Neddy') and the National
Incomes Commission ('Nicky'), on which representatives from industry and the
unions sat with Ministers and Civil Servants to try to plan the nation's economy
as well as to regulate wages. This, of course, was the complete reversal of the
slogan of the 1951 election which had been 'Set the people free'. Macmillan, with
his ideas on planning and regulation, had set the Party leftwards again, in a
socialist direction.

Macmillan and the Commonwealth

Churchill had promised the maintenance of the Empire; Eden had tried to
reassert the power of Britain; Macmillan was more astute than his predecessors.
He realised that if the majority of people in, say, Ghana, Kenya, Tanganyika—or
any other colonial country—demanded their independence then Britain had two
alternatives: she could refuse to agree to the demand, face the consequent uprising
with an army and go through the bitter experience of arresting and imprisoning
the leaders; or she could accept that in the 1950s Britain no long had the power
to assert her authority over unwilling subjects, particularly since world opinion
in the UNO and diplomatic and financial pressure from the USA would work
against her.

It is a mark of Macmillan's ability that he managed to turn the Party leftwards
in this as in economic thinking, without breaking the Party. Ghana (1957),
Malaya (1957), Cyprus (1960), Nigeria (1960), Tanganyika and Zanzibar (1960),
Sierra Leone (1961), and Kenya (1963) were given their independence by the
Macmillan government. The Central African Federation of Rhodesia, Nyasaland
and Zambia was broken up in 1963 and Zambia and Malawi (Nyasaland)
became independent countries ruled over by African politicians. Only Southern
Rhodesia with its white-dominated government did not get its independence. The
Conservative government insisted on maintaining some control over that country
until the African majority had been allowed a share in the governing process.

The retreat from Empire was a recognition both of Britain's decline and of the

57 Macmillan with Sir Roy Welensky, then Prime Minister of the Rhodesian Federation of
Southern Rhodesia and Nyasaland. One of Macmillan's great achievements was to persuade the
Conservative Party and the British people to give up their African Empire

right of people to govern themselves. It was this belief that lay behind one of Macmillan's most famous speeches. Early in 1960 he toured Africa; his last port of call was South Africa. Macmillan addressed the white South African Parliament and outlined to them the changes that he could see were taking place on the vast Continent of Africa. In many countries in the North, the East and the West of Africa, former colonial territories had become, or were going to become, independent. The black man was no longer subject to the white man; this said Macmillan was the 'wind of change' that was blowing through Africa—and he argued that the white South Africans had better take this into account in their dealings with their own black people.

Britain and Europe

One of the major triumphs of Macmillan's period of office was that he converted the Conservative Party from being an imperialist–minded party to being a party which saw Britain's future as one of partnership with European countries in the European Economic Community (EEC, or Common Market). This conversion was a long and slow process. In 1955 a Conference was held at Messina, in Italy, to work out a scheme for creating a new Europe. As Nora Beloff wrote, in *The General Says No*, the British government was not interested in this idea of unity:

> Neither Macmillan nor anyone else in the Eden government saw any reason to get excited. . . . The only important thing was that the Six were now talking about trade; the Board of Trade, it was felt, should find out what was happening. . . . Britain sent an official from the Board of Trade, Mr Bretherton. . . . He was told to make the Europeans understand that if they were again up to their supranational tricks they could not expect Whitehall to take them seriously. . . . Bretherton outlined the reasons for Britain's apprehension, her opposition to any arrangement which might collide with her Commonwealth commitment and her insistence that the Community must remain inside the OEEC framework. . . . Only that happened to be the last time British officials were invited to any Brussels meetings. Mr Bretherton packed his bags and went home . . . Britain had nothing more to do with negotiating with the Common Market.

However, the British were interested in the idea of a reduction in tariffs which could lead to increased trade—provided that Britain was still allowed to retain her links with the Commonwealth which provided Britain with cheap food. Macmillan was opposed to the EEC: but he did help to create a new trading agreement with seven European countries (EFTA) and he hoped to persuade the six (EEC) countries to join with EFTA in creating a Europe free from internal tariffs between member countries. In May 1957 Reginald Maudling represented the government in trying to persuade the other European countries to adopt a free trade area.

The members of the EEC saw this as an attempt by Britain to get the best of both worlds—to have free trade inside Europe to which Britain could sell her manufactured goods while retaining her preferential arrangements with the

Commonwealth which gave her the cheap food—so preventing French, German and other farmers gaining a foothold in the British market. By 1962 the British economy was in another of its crises while the economies of the EEC countries continued to expand so that their people's standard of living continued to rise, and for the first time German, French and Belgian workers began to enjoy a higher standard of living than their British counterparts. Maybe, after all, there was something to be said in favour of European unity.

In a speech to the Conservative Party Conference in October 1962, Macmillan announced that he was going to try to get Britain into Europe. Edward Heath, from the Board of Trade, was sent to Brussels to negotiate with the EEC representatives. Britain seemed quite prepared to turn her back on the Commonwealth, to expose her own agriculture to European competition, to accept the price of a high tariff on food which would mean a rise in the cost of living. However, General de Gaulle, the French President, was still not assured that Britain was really converted to the European idea, and he vetoed her application; it was a shock from which the Macmillan government never recovered.

58 From left to right—Edward Heath, Duncan Sandys and Christopher Soames with Dr Schroder, the German Foreign Minister, after the announcement in January 1963 that General de Gaulle had vetoed Britain's application to join the Common Market

Party unpopularity

Macmillan had been a very successful leader, as one of his Cabinet colleagues, the Earl of Swinton, recalled:

> How can we assess his Premiership? Harold's own parable about the 'five balls in the air' provides the secret to the achievements with which his era is identified. First, political union and recovery.... Second, economic expansion and social well-being.... Third, restore the Anglo-American partnership so disastrously ruptured by Suez.... Fourth, thaw the East-West cold war.... Fifth, the 'wind of change' in Africa.... And to these I would add not the least imaginative, his conception of Britain's entry into the Common Market.
> *(From 'Sixty Years of Power', by the Earl of Swinton, published 1966 by Hutchinson.)*

But in 1962 the picture changed. The decline in the economy led to a rise in unemployment. One of the reasons for Macmillan's popularity in 1959 was that people had 'never had it so good'. As David Butler writes, the opposite was true of 1962—depression brought political unpopularity:

59 Macmillan was too ill to attend the Party Conference in October 1963. When he sent a message from hospital to say that he was going to retire the Conference became a centre of intrigue and speculation as to who would succeed him as Prime Minister. Many assumed that this time Butler, still deputy Prime Minister, would get his chance. Others favoured Edward Heath (second from the left) and a few liberal Tories supported the claims of Iain Macleod (far right). In fact, the little-fancied Lord Home (centre, with hands raised) got the job

On 12 July at Leicester North-West by-election the Conservative candidate finished an ignominious third, 10 per cent behind the Liberal. The next day the Chancellor of the Exchequer was sacked along with the Lord Chancellor and five other Cabinet Ministers. Many believed Macmillan was 'mainly acting in desperation because of the government's recent by-election defeats'. . . . On 14 January 1963 [President de Gaulle] indicated that his country could no longer support Britain's application for EEC membership.

. . . The number of unemployed rose to 2.5 per cent of the labour force in December 1962; in February 1963 the total reached 3.9 per cent. . . . The number who feared unemployment was even higher. . . . During the late winter Conservative murmurings against Mr Macmillan's leadership could be heard. (*From 'The British General Election of 1964', by Butler and King published by Macmillan.*)

The Party was prepared to have Macmillan as leader while he was successful. Nothing failed him like failure in the eyes of the Party and in 1963 they were glad to have his resignation. He was succeeded by the fourteenth Earl of Home who gave up his title to become Sir Alec Douglas Home. Was the Party trying to turn itself into an aristocratic party again? Was it going to turn its back on the Baldwin-Macmillan idea of a leftwards-looking Party which sought the middle ground of political ideas?

10　Heath and a New Era?

Out of office

In 1964 the Conservative Party was defeated in the general election. Led by Sir Alec Douglas Home the Conservatives won 304 seats at the 1964 election to Labour's 317 seats, the Liberals gaining 9. In spite of the electoral unpopularity the Party nearly gained its fourth consecutive electoral victory. If it had done so perhaps the Macmillan brand of Conservatism would have been pursued. But the Labour victory of 1964, followed by a second success in 1966 (by 363 seats to 253 for the Conservatives) convinced many Conservatives that the Party had to rethink its ideas.

One of the reasons for Labour's success was the emergence of Harold Wilson as Labour's leader, with his appeal to the young technologists and technicians of industrial Britain. He made it appear that the Labour Party was the one which would ensure Britain's success in the modern world of 'white-hot technology', and that if planning and regulation were required to run a modern economy then

60　On Home's retirement the Party chose Edward Heath (left) as leader. He relied to a great extent on the experienced and able Iain Macleod whose death just after the Conservative victory in the 1970 election was a great blow to liberalism and to the Party

61 James Prior (left) Minister of Agriculture in the Heath government with Peter Walker, who, at thirty-eight, was the youngest member of the Cabinet

the Labour Party was the one best suited to do this. Thus the Labour Party held on to its traditional working-class support but also gained the electoral support of many members of the middle class.

Selsdon man

Edward Heath succeeded Sir Alec Douglas Home as Party leader in 1965. He set up a number of working parties to examine the reasons for the Party's failure in the elections of 1964 and 1966; he also asked these working parties to produce reports showing how the Party might govern in the future. One of the noticeable things about the people who took charge of these working parties was that few, if any, of them belonged to the older, traditional, rich Conservative section of the community. Instead, Mr Heath asked younger people to take charge—people such as Peter Walker who seemed to represent Heath's idea of the modern Conservative. Mr Walker had none of the traditional Conservative advantages— he did not go to a public school or to Oxford or Cambridge. After leaving grammar school he had worked in an insurance firm until, in his mid–twenties, he decided to launch a new savings scheme of his own. This had attracted a good deal of public support and money, and Mr Walker had become a very wealthy man; in alliance with another similarly forceful young man, Jim Slater, Walker had gone into the property market and made himself even richer.

In some ways, the story is that of Mr Heath's own life. He was the son of a working man and gained a scholarship from his grammar school to Oxford; he made his way in the Party through hard work, being promoted by Macmillan to the Board of Trade. The Heath-Walker solution to Britain's problems seemed to be self-help.

The Party leaders held a series of conferences at a large hotel in Selsdon Park, near Croydon, to consider the reports from their various working parties and committees. These reports—on the Welfare State, taxation, education, nationalised industries and so on—were then linked together in a further series of papers and reports, which in turn were considered at more meetings at Selsdon Park. From this long consideration there came a series of simpler pamphlets and leaflets to be used by candidates and other speakers who were to outline Party policy to the Party workers and the electorate.

The theme that seemed to run through the documents was that in the past Britain had become a highly taxed nation in which the hard work of managers and other highly paid people was not sufficiently rewarded—since the tax man took away a good deal of their income. This, said the new Conservatism, would have to change; taxation would have to be brought down. To do this, the government would have to restrict its role as nursemaid in the Welfare State—people

62 John Davies, Secretary of State for Industry in the Heath government in 1970, and the author of the phrase 'lame ducks' as a description of industries and areas which the government would no longer help. With him is Lord Carrington, Minister for Defence—who was used by Heath as a trouble shooter in Ireland, Malta, Singapore and elsewhere

would have to pay for some of the benefits which in the past they had got for nothing or for less than cost. So, for example, the customer would have to pay more for medicines and dental treatment, for school meals and council houses—and this would allow the government to reduce taxation. The successful man would be allowed to retain more of his money.

The Conservatives also promised to give less aid to British industry than in the past; there would be less help from a Conservative government for declining industries and areas. If an industry was making a loss and could not pay its way, the Conservatives would not bail it out by a government grant. Just as the individual had to stand on his own feet (and not get free school meals, milk or medicines) so industry would have to stand on its own feet without government assistance. This was a reversal of the Baldwin-Macmillan trend.

Government again

In June 1970 Mr Heath led the Conservatives to a victory over the Labour Party, gaining 330 seats to Labour's 287, the Liberals winning only 6 seats. In his government, the bright young men had a large sway—Peter Walker was made Minister for the Environment, one of the new super-Ministries, taking in the former Ministries of Transport, Local Government, Housing, and several others. The successful businessmen were represented by John Davies, formerly the Secretary of the Confederation of British Industry—a sort of trade union of industrialists. It was John Davies who won the largest applause from the Party Conference held just after the 1970 election when he said that the government would not help the loss-making industries. These 'lame ducks', as he called them, and also the declining regions, had to stand on their own feet—or fall.

And at first the government did what it said. Mrs Thatcher, as Minister of Education, announced the abolition of free school milk for children over the age of seven—and was christened 'Thatcher the Snatcher'; Sir Keith Joseph, in charge of the Health Service, announced a large increase in charges to be paid by patients for medicine and other treatment; John Davies, at the super-Ministry of Trade and Industry, announced the abolition of the help previously given to the old industrialised areas such as the North East and South Wales, Scotland and the North West. So in his first Budget, Anthony Barber was able to reduce taxation by over £100 million.

But within a short time the government was in full retreat. Perhaps the most spectacular withdrawal was that made by John Davies in the matter of Rolls Royce; this giant firm, producer of most of the world's aero-engines, had contracted to produce an engine for Lockheed—an American firm. By 1971 it had found that it could not produce the engine on time, which would involve the company in paying huge sums in penalties for non-delivery, and would also be unable to produce it for the agreed figure. Rolls-Royce, one of Britain's proudest names, had to announce that it was bankrupt, unable to meet its debts to Lockheeds and its other customers who had supplied it with the materials to produce the engine which Lockheed were refusing to buy at the higher price. The government

89

64 Upper Clyde Shipyard workers refused to accept the government's decision to close down their yards—as part of the 'lame duck' policy (picture 68). Led by Jimmy Reid (second from the left) and James Airlie (on Reid's left), they organised a work-in which forced the government to change its policies. Here they can be seen on 16 June 1971 outside 10 Downing Street, where they went to see Prime Minister Heath

stepped in, nationalised the firm, and took over responsibility for its debts; this was a major turn-round in policy. 'Lame ducks' were to be helped after all.

Perhaps the most humiliating withdrawal was made in the case of the Upper Clyde Shipbuilders, a firm which had been getting government assistance for over twenty years to try to maintain employment in the Glasgow area, which already had a high level of unemployment. The Conservative government refused to increase the level of this grant and announced that the firm was bankrupt and that four shipyards would have to close down, with about 20,000 men being thrown out of work. But the men, led by their shop stewards, refused to accept this decision; they occupied the yards, continued to build the ships that were there and mobilised public opinion until the government was forced to announce that, whereas it would not give £6 million in 1971, in 1972 it was prepared to give

63 Anthony Barber who succeeded Macleod as Chancellor (Picture 66) outside his official home, 11 Downing St. with the Budget Bag on Budget Day, 1971

£40 million to keep the yards open, to modernise them and invite an American firm to take them over.

Indeed, by June 1972 the government seemed to have undone all that it had promised, and done the very things which it had tried to undo; it became more actively engaged in guiding the economy than the Labour government ever was; it spent more on assistance to industry and distressed areas than Labour ever did— only Mrs Thatcher's milk policy remained unchanged.

Conclusion

Macmillan had commented on the change in thinking that had taken place during his lifetime. The Heath government seemed to be anxious to reverse that trend towards conservative-socialism which had characterised the Macmillan period. But the price for this reversal was found to be too high by the winter of 1971, when there were over 1 million people unemployed—the highest figure since the depressed 1930s. It seemed that if a government does not play an active part in the nation's economic and social life then unemployment is a result—and public opinion turns against a government which allows unemployment to rise. The Party seems to be committed inevitably to increasingly socialist policies since this is what breeds electoral success.

65 A 'Garland' cartoon of 31 March 1972. From left to right: Sir Alec Douglas Home (Foreign Secretary), Lord Carrington (Minister for Defence), John Davies (Industry and Trade), Robert Carr (Minister for Employment) and William Whitelaw (the Party's Chief Whip). They are shown trying to plug the leaks in the dyke marked Tory policies. After only two years the policies which the Heath government had hoped to implement had been shown to be either unworkable or unacceptable

Further Reading

General studies of the history of political parties

THOMAS, IVOR BULMER	*The Growth of the British Party System*	Baker
MACKENZIE, R. T.	*British Political Parties*	Heinemann
JENNINGS, SIR IVOR	*Party Politics—the Growth of Parties*	C.U.P.

The Conservative Party

BLAKE, R.	*The Conservative Party from Peel to Churchill*	Methuen
CLARK, G. KITSON	*Peel and the Conservative Party*	Cass, F.
WHITE, R. J. (ED.)	*The Conservative Tradition*	Black

Memoirs or Autobiographies

GORE, J. (ED.)	*The Creevey Papers*	John Murray
CHURCHILL, SIR WINSTON	*Memoirs*	Macmillan
MACMILLAN, HAROLD	*Memoirs*	Macmillan
LORD AVON (ANTHONY EDEN)	*Memoirs*	Macmillan
BEVINS, R.	*The Greasy Pole*	Hodder & Stoughton

Biographies

BROCK, W. R.	*Lord Liverpool and Liberal Toryism*	Cass, F.
BLAKE, R.	*Disraeli*	Methuen
KENNEDY, A.	*Salisbury*	John Murray
JAMES, R. R.	*Lord Randolph Churchill*	Weidenfeld & Nicolson
CHURCHILL, RANDOLPH	*Lord Derby*	Heinemann
BLAKE, R.	*Bonar Law, the Unknown Prime Minister*	Methuen
MIDDLEMAS and BARNES	*Baldwin*	Weidenfeld & Nicolson
MACLEOD, IAIN	*Neville Chamberlain*	Muller

Topics

For general background see the Pelican *History of England* for each of the Seventeenth, Eighteenth and Nineteenth Centuries

BRIGGS, ASA	*The Age of Improvement —1783–1867*	Longman
WHITE, R. J.	*From Waterloo to Peterloo*	Penguin
DISRAELI	*Sybil, Coningsby*	Penguin
JENKINS, R.	*Mr Balfour's Poodle*	Heinemann
GRAVES and HODGE	*The Long Weekend*	Penguin
BOOKER, C.	*The Neophiliacs*	Collins

Index